M000198610

Making 1/12 Scale
CHARACTER
FIGURES

Making 1/12 Scale
CHARACTER
FIGURES

James Carrington

GUILD OF MASTER CRAFTSMAN PUBLICATIONS

20006871
MORAY COUNCIL
Department of Technical
& Leisure Services
745·592.

First published 2000 by
Guild of Master Craftsman Publications Ltd,
166 High Street, Lewes,
East Sussex, BN7 1XU

Text and illustrations copyright © James Carrington 2000
Copyright in the work © Guild of Master Craftsman Publications Ltd

ISBN 1 86108 161 8

All rights reserved

The right of James Carrington to be identified as the author of this work has been asserted in
accordance with the Copyright Designs and Patents Act 1988, Sections 77 and 78.

No part of this publication may be reproduced, stored in a retrieval system, or transmitted in any
form or by any means without the prior permission of the publisher and copyright owner.

This book is sold subject to the condition that all designs are copyright and are not for
commercial reproduction without the written permission of the designer and copyright owner.

The publishers and authors can accept no legal responsibility for any consequences arising from
the application of information, advice or instructions given in this publication.

A catalogue record of this book is available from the British Library.

Dolls' house accessories available from
The London Dolls' House Company, Covent Garden, London, England.

Tools available worldwide by mail order from Alec Tiranti Limited, 70 High Street, Theale,
Berkshire, RG7 5AR, England. Email: enquiries@tiranti.co.uk.

Sets available from Steve Hilbert of Chapel Road, 47 Chapel Road, Bexleyheath, Kent, England.

Cover photograph, figure photography and step by step photography by Gary Sinfield

Author photograph by Bruce Mackay

Additional step by step photography, cut outs of figures and illustrations by James Carrington

Designed by Paul Griffin

Typeface: Palatino

Colour origination by Viscan Graphics (Singapore)
Printed in China by Sun Fung Offset Binding Co., Ltd.

To Mary Mawson
with love

Contents

 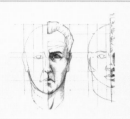

INTRODUCTION

T*HEY SAY THAT confession is good for the soul and since I hope that, like me, you never read introductions, this seems like a good place to hide one. In a secret corner of my workshop is a box of my early figures. I can't believe that I actually thought that they were passable as human beings – and I love them dearly. They teach me that the figures I make today are the result of many experiments and many more mistakes. No figure is wasted as long as you are learning how to do it better next time. The important thing is to keep trying. I love the idea of the Turkish rug makers who build into their work deliberate mistakes so as not to offend Allah. Only a deity can do absolute perfection – we may try, but can never truly succeed.*

*Knowing this, we can start out on the quest to create the **nearly** perfect figure. But wait, think, has your head told you that you can't do it? Perhaps you think it would actually be easier to make a cake or clean the kitchen floor? Well, here's a trick I was taught; it's called the irreducible minimum. Let me ask you a question. How do you start a letter? Do you write your address, or start with 'Dear so*

Kitchen Chaos

Kitchen Gossip

and so...'? Try the irreducible minimum way of doing it – get a pen and paper. First things first. The same applies to doll making. Read the chapter you want to work on, set out the tools and then you can start. Don't project on what you think you can't do. Surprise yourself and have a try, it's much easier than you think.

Remember that this is my way of making lifelike figures; it's by no means the only way. There will be certain rules, but they are only there to guide you, and once learned, can be broken if it suits your way better. We each have our own style, and a particular type of face will always appeal to each and every one of us. It's up to you to discover the type that is yours. With me, I have always drawn and modelled a 'well-nosed', thin face with a high, sloping forehead, and it has often puzzled me as to where it came from. Then, on a visit to Spain, I saw the Catalan face, and it felt like coming home. Perhaps, in a past life I was from that region of the country. I do make many other heads, but that particular one is precious to me.

The methods described in this book are simple and need very little initial outlay, although the thought of buying good tools at the start may seem a bit excessive, I promise you that it's a good investment, and you will find a million and one other uses for them. The main aim is to have fun and be spontaneous. Don't think of each one as being a separate entity. Think of the story line you want them to convey, how each will interact with another, and plan for the future. As you work and get better, you will want to replace your original models with finer figures. Nothing need ever be wasted; plan a room setting for a Museum of Waxworks or Chamber of Horrors and relegate those early ones to the role of exhibits? You could place a couple of your newer figures into the scene, laughing at the feeble attempts of the owner.

Once you have started, you are halfway to finishing your first figure.

Have fun!

Setting up a
WORK STATION

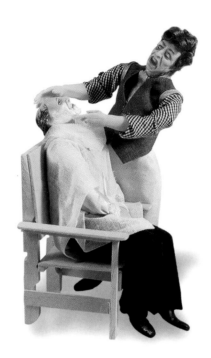

Sweeney Todd and Judge Turpin

B<small>Y FAR THE BEST WAY</small> *of learning to make figures is to have a work station you can call your own. If you are new to the hobby of miniatures, you will have to learn some basic skills, especially if you share your home with other individuals who may not share your addiction. How they never understand that a hobby that started out with a box with doors and windows, happily sitting in the corner of a room, can have escalated into an obsession that threatens to take over the whole house is beyond me. The skill is to train them.*

You will learn in time that most makers fully understand that you need two receipts – one to show, the other to hide. (This applies to both sexes.) And that take-aways come with very useful containers, and therefore save money in the long run. When it comes to something like making your own figures, it's easy. Drag your partner to a major fair and show them "the astronomic price we charge" for something you could do with a little practice that "won't take up any space at all". Be single-minded, and stick to your guns.

Claim some space to work in and return to whenever you want. There is nothing better to put yourself off doing a job than having continually to set up the table again and again. I have a studio to work in, but even with that space it takes me a good ten minutes every morning to find where I left my glasses the night before, plug the phone in, and find the scissors (yes, I do have other ones around the house, but the pair in the studio are the ones I like to use best). It's called procrastination, and I play it every day of my life. I've also learned that it's part of my setting-up routine, and in its own way, is part of how I work best.

In fact, at first you need very little space to make the figures, so if you can't claim a permanent space, set up a large tray which you can move to one side without having to disturb your work, and return where you left off.

Work in as good a natural light as you can, but if you have to work under electric light have at least two light sources, one from either side of your work. You can make your own choice as to whether to use normal bulbs, spotlights or daylight bulbs. I find the latter uncomfortable to work under – they are too cold a colour – but, then, I do have a good supply of natural daylight. You may also find an illuminated magnifier useful; it all depends on your own eyesight.

By having a workspace of your own, you will find that your work flows more easily, and you end up with something to justify your space much more quickly – and the family will be pleased. Well, that's the thought, some are more difficult to train than others.

At my work station

Materials and EQUIPMENT

Scarlet Woman, Courtesan and Busybody

Waiting For Work

MODELLING

POLYMER CLAY

All polymer clays are basically the same but some grades contain a higher resin content, and the higher the resin content, the stronger the finished result. These clays are sold in large packs, are more economical and, although harder to start off, give a far superior finished product. Most of the small packs are available in a flesh colour but beware, these can yellow in daylight over time.

Most of you will perhaps have a specific preference for a brand and it's a good idea to stick with it; you can move over to another one later if you decide you'd like to experiment. The ones most figure makers tend to use, and which are quite accessible, are as follows:

PUPPEN FIMO

This is available in 500g packs. A German product made specifically for dolls, it has a good basic flesh colour, and is firm to handle. It can be ordered easily from any art stores selling Fimo products.

You will normally use acrylic-based paints for painting your figures, but note that oil-based paints do not respond very well to this brand of clay, often remaining tacky to the touch for long periods of time, for ever in fact.

SUPER SCULPEY

An American product, this is widely available from art stores in the larger size 1lb packs. Like the Puppen Fimo, it is flesh-coloured, but also has a slightly translucent finish. It is nice and soft to handle, but can be a little fragile when it is baked.

Polymer clay

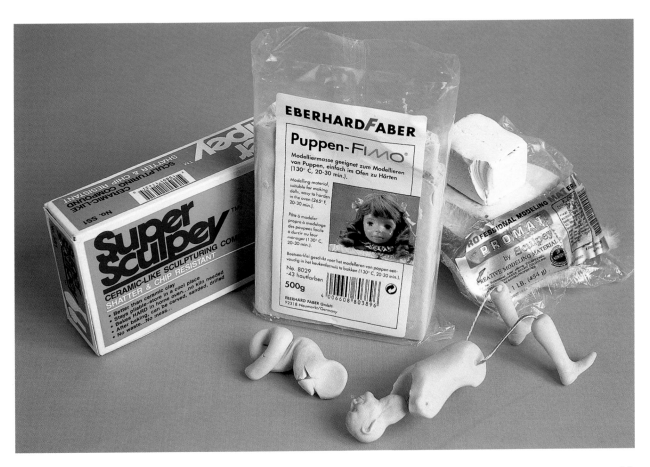

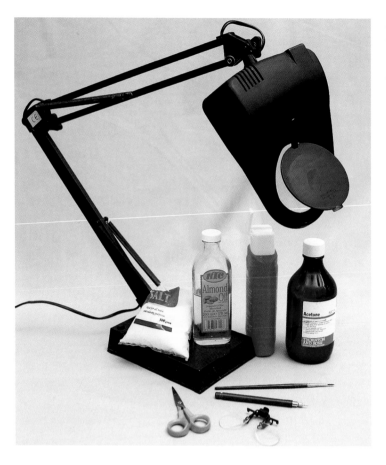

A selection of materials and equipment for figure making

HANDLING THE CLAY

The first rule is, work with clean hands. No, I'm not suggesting anything, but you will be surprised just how much the clay picks up. Try this before you start. Pour some oil into your hands and rub in, then pour over some salt and wring your hands together really well. I know it sounds lethal but if you use almond oil, it will nourish your nails. Now wash off with soap and water. Your hands will be very slippery,so be prepared to rescue the soap when it shoots through your fingers.

USING THE CLAY

The best way to find out how your clay responds is to practise. Try not to do this on the figure to start with, it will make you nervous. Set up any tools that you have, and work some clay to really soften it. Take a piece and add a blob of clay to the surface. Take any one of your tools and see if it spreads over the clay to unite the surfaces. Wooden tools are usually best for this job. Try not to spread it like butter, but pat and pull the edges backwards and forwards to amalgamate them.

Try the metal tools out and see what each

SCULPEY PROMAT

This is available in 1lb packs. It is white and has a strong finish. It has a tendency to become slack with working. Oil-based paints work well on this clay.

An oven timer and oven thermometer are useful when baking your clay

TIPS

1) Do not eat, drink or smoke while using the clay.

2) Use an oven thermometer to check the temperature of your oven. There are different ones to choose from, and having one will ensure a successful result. Check it regularly as thermostats can sometimes get a bit 'out' with age.

3) Keep a timer handy, the phone is bound to ring. And please take the figures out as soon as they are done. I once left a whole batch in, forgot about it, and later turned the oven back on high to do some Yorkshire puddings. Needless to say, it was gruesome, frustrating, and could have been very dangerous.

is capable of. Don't expect one tool to do every job.

Work on something other than a face or a hand, perhaps a cabbage or a rose (my roses look like cabbages, anyway), otherwise you will concentrate more on getting the face or hand right and forget that you are learning to use the clay and tools in combination.

STORAGE

Store the clay in its wrapper, and no other plastics. If you do, the molecules can pass from one to the other and ruin the clay. Likewise, don't store or rest the clay for too long on paper; this dries out the oils which keep the clay supple. For best results, work and bake the clay on a ceramic tile (at least, not on anything you may wish to eat from!).

BAKING

Instructions for baking time vary with each product, so check the pack for details. Use an oven thermometer to check the oven temperature. There is a variety to choose from on the market, but whichever one you buy it will ensure a successful result. (It will also give you better cakes and roasts.) In addition, it is a good idea to use an oven timer; the phone is bound to ring.

ADDITIONAL MATERIALS

ACETONE
(TO FINISH THE SURFACE OF THE CLAY)

MOULD MAKING

PLASTER

Avoid at all costs the sort of plaster you get from the chemist or builder's yard; these are intended for mending broken limbs and building walls. You need plaster with a slow cure, so that it stays in liquid form for a reasonable time and has a hard finish. Look up plaster suppliers in your local phone book, or ask a local dental technician for one. I recommend Kaffir 'D'.

ADDITIONAL MATERIALS

PARTING AGENT (PETROLEUM JELLY, SILICON SPRAY OR COOKING OIL)
MODELLING CLAY OR PLASTICINE
TALCUM POWDER (TO ACT AS A RELEASING AGENT WHEN TAKING A PULL FROM A MOULD)

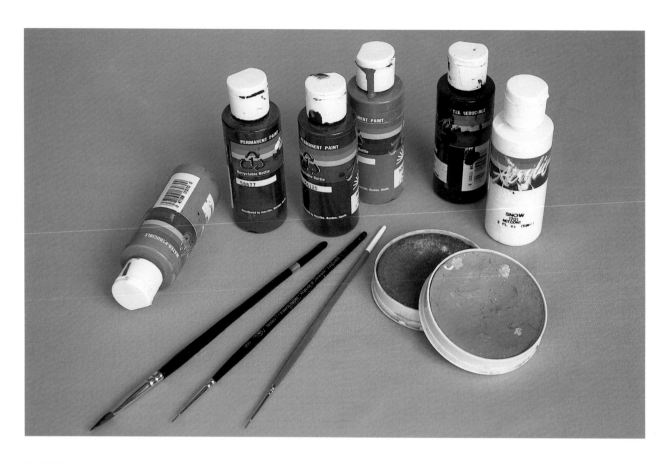

Use good quality paintbrushes for painting your character figures

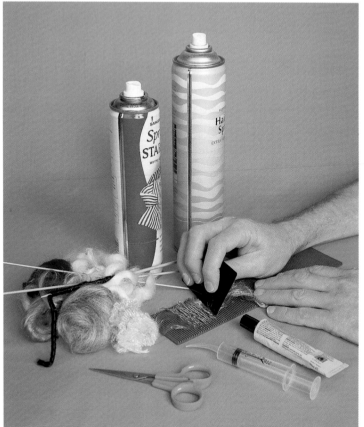

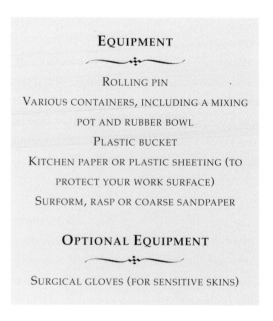

EQUIPMENT

ROLLING PIN

VARIOUS CONTAINERS, INCLUDING A MIXING

POT AND RUBBER BOWL

PLASTIC BUCKET

KITCHEN PAPER OR PLASTIC SHEETING (TO

PROTECT YOUR WORK SURFACE)

SURFORM, RASP OR COARSE SANDPAPER

OPTIONAL EQUIPMENT

SURGICAL GLOVES (FOR SENSITIVE SKINS)

Everything you need for wigging

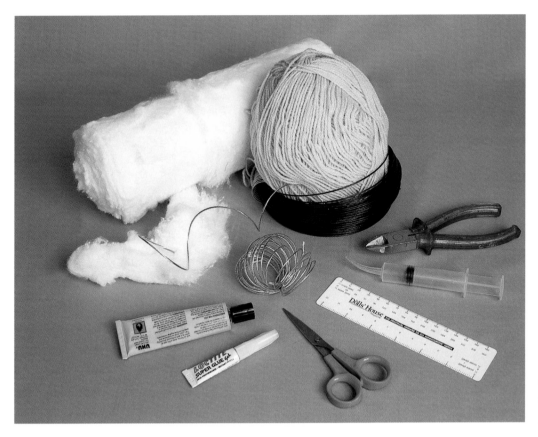

Materials and equipment for filling in limbs

ASSEMBLY AND FINISHING

AQUACOLOR

This theatrical foundation colour, is widely available in a solid block, and needs water added to use. The glycerine base to this product neutralizes any oil still remaining in the clay after baking, and prepares the surface of the clay for water-based acrylic paints. The translucent quality of the Aquacolor gives natural-looking extra shadow in the creases and hollows of the face and hands.

PAINT

Acrylic paints are ideal if you have primed the surface with the foundation colour first. The alternative is to wash the surface with water and a very tiny drop of washing-up liquid and dry with a paper towel. I do mean a tiny drop; you don't want the paint to foam up, do you?

I have found that acrylic paint is by far the best to use on clay, but be aware that some products have a tendency to scratch off easily; even a series of colours may have one or two in their range that do not want to fix. Check as you work that this does not happen. Sometimes manufacturers change their formula and an acrylic colour that has been perfect previously, can now seem to be useless.

The other safe alternative is artist's watercolour paint, widely available in small blocks. Although it seems at first to be very fragile, it can give quite a permanent finish if it is treated with care. You can use spray varnish to fix it, but even the most matt finish will give a sheen to the face of the figure.

HAIR

There are two basic types of hair suitable for miniature work.

15

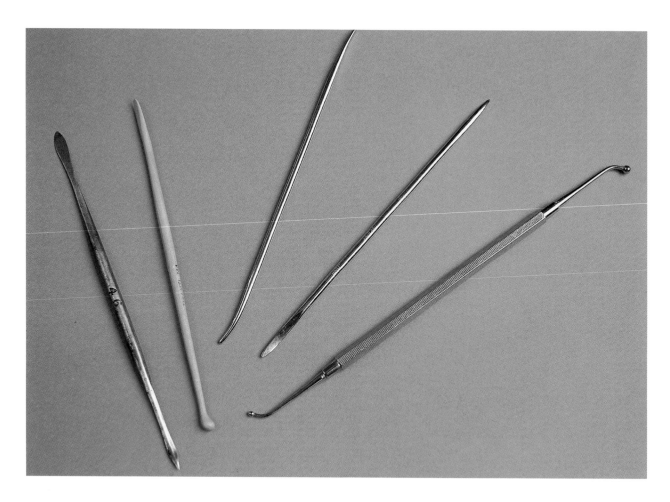

Good tools beget good work. These are the five essential sculpting tools

VISCOSE

I prefer the viscose in its straight form. It is available in other forms, too; some that shrink when heated, and some that are available in the curl, but plain and simple works for me. Because viscose is man-made and the dye is very uniform, it is best to mix two shades to get a more realistic colour.

MOHAIR AND SUPERFINE MOHAIR

Mohair in its finest state can work for some people, and is good when you want to do a period 'wig' because these were made of horsehair. The slightly coarser fibre can work well, but is harder to curl and to get the curl to stay in place. Being natural hair, the slightest wisp of moisture can relax the hair straight again. The advantage of mohair is its more natural colour range.

SCULPTING TOOLS

There is a saying that a bad workman always blames his tools, but I believe that a good workman only uses good tools in the first place. I used to think that when I became really good at sculpture I would invest in proper tools and then realized that if I started right I would continue to get better. Good tools beget good work, though I know many figure makers who swear by tooth picks.

In my workbox I now have a range of five essential tools which feel like they are part of my hand, and I just couldn't work comfortably without them.

I have one warning for you, however: beware the great tidy up. I once lost a tool doing this and it took me weeks to train the new one.

TOOL 46

This is a very basic, 'rough and ready' metal tool with a thin spatula end, good for trimming, cutting and smoothing, and has a pointed end for scratching in lines. It is very useful for mould making. File the spatula end down if it gets a burr on it (like every time you drop it).

TOOL 104–330 M4

This is the perfect wooden tool. Wood is particularly good for amalgamating edges of clay together. The clay has a tendency to adhere to the wood and this helps carry a trace of clay from one edge to another. The flat end does the smoothing, is great for separating the fingers, and for basic work

on the eyes. The ball end creates hollows on the face, neck and palm of the hand.

TOOL 103–180 DM14

This is a very fine metal modelling tool. It has a flat, almond-shaped end for cutting in lines around the eyes and the mouth. It is excellent for cleaning and smoothing out flat areas.

TOOL 103–170 DM13

This is a double-ended pointed tool, one end slightly larger than the other, with rounded backs, and is the one I cannot live without. It is the ultimate detail tool – the points make fingernails, mark the eyeball, make nostrils, and create wrinkles and

Using a wooden tool to fill in a solid arm

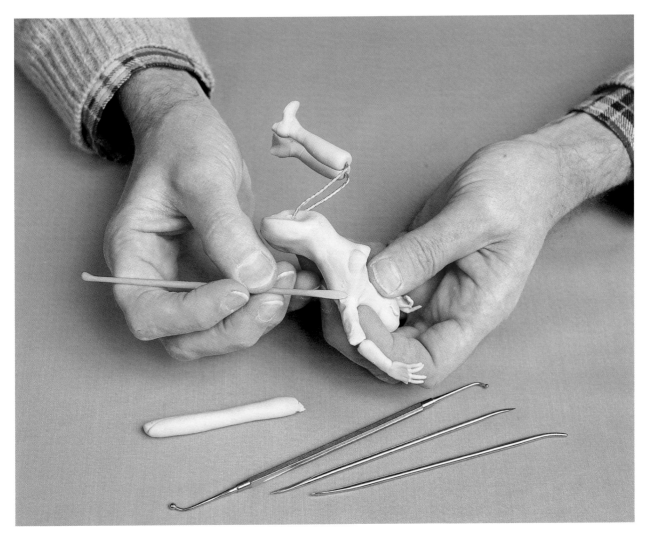

lines. You name a detail and this tool will do it. The rounded backs shape the lips, smooth fingers and any tight areas. It is good for digging clay out from under your nails, too.

TOOL 103–040 SD

This is actually a dental tool. It is a double-ended ball tool of different sizes, which defines the nose, eye bags, chin, and other areas of the face. It is good, too, for adding more detail to hollows on the hands and face. It is also great for doing ears (the doll's, not yours).

For other sources and advice, seek out a sculpture supplier, or ask a dental technician or local art college.

BRUSHES

You have two choices of brush: sable or synthetic. Sable is a natural animal product and some may find it ethically unacceptable. We have to hope that the synthetic variety is at least environmentally friendly. Because sable is natural hair, it has a texture which holds paint better and has a more natural spring to it, but other products are getting better all the time and it is no bad thing to experiment occasionally. The cost of sable is higher than synthetic.

Allow yourself to be very fussy when buying brushes of whichever sort. There was a time when art stores would supply the customer with a pot of water to try each one out, but in the absence of this service

Painting on the foundation colour with a good quality sable brush

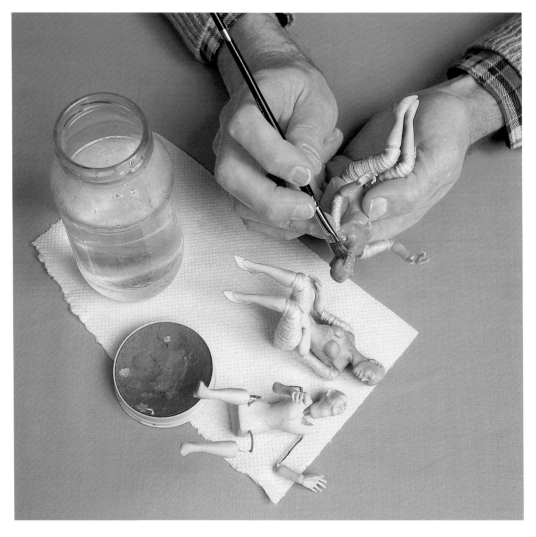

ADDITIONAL EQUIPMENT

SUPERGLUE

GENERAL ADHESIVE

MEDIUM-WEIGHT BRASS PICTURE WIRE OR

PLASTIC-COATED GARDEN WIRE

COTTON WOOL

KNITTING WOOL (FLESH COLOUR)

SMALL PAIR OF SCISSORS

(PARTICULARLY USEFUL FOR CUTTING

THE FIGURE'S FINGERS)

RULER

GLUE SYRINGE

WIRE CUTTERS

PINS (FOR SECURING LIMBS)

ELECTRIC (PREFERABLY CORDLESS)

OR HAND DRILL

OPTIONAL EQUIPMENT

ILLUMINATED MAGNIFIER

(FOR DETAIL, AND FOR THOSE WHO HAVE

POOR EYESIGHT)

To keep the brushes in good condition, pay them some respect. Do not leave paint on the brush to dry, and use a separate pot of clean water to wash them in as you are using them. That means keeping two water pots – one for painting and the other one for rinsing out your brushes.

At the end of the day, wash the brushes with care in soapy water, pinch out the clean water between the folds of a paper towel, run the brush over a piece of soap and smooth the hairs into a point. This will 'starch' the hairs and pull the brush back into a good shape. Just remember to rinse out the soap before you next start to paint. You will need at least a No. 000 sable brush (or good synthetic alternative) for painting the face, and a No. 3 for cleaning with acetone and general work. You will also need another soft brush.

Materials and equipment for making a mould

I've been known to suck the bristles to see if they have been lain properly. This is not a thing I would recommend you do (in case you get into trouble), but do take them out of their protective tube and roll the length of the brush across a piece of paper. Quite often you will find that the finishing off leaves the tips with a tiny curl, and they never, ever, straighten out.

Having invested in new brushes, don't expect them to last a lifetime; throw them away when they look like they are past their prime. I do try to convince myself that I will find some use for old brushes and waste ages sorting through the old ones to find the new ones. I do know, though, that it's the law that the moment I do have a clear out, I will find a use for them.

A note about
OBSERVATION

The Wind Trio

W E ALL LIKE TO BELIEVE THAT *we have a very sophisticated brain, but when it comes to observation we have progressed very little since the Stone Age. Our brains take in an enormous amount, but we register very little. We 'see' what we need to survive. When we look at another person we need to know whether they are friend or foe, attractive to us or not, etc. Our eyes scan the face and body for clues at a rapid rate and compute the information in an instant, and this gives us all the basic information required. If you think of the number of people that you meet in a day, it's a good job that this is done at such speed, otherwise we'd never be able get on with anything else.*

The art of observation has to be learned, and this comes with daily practice. We have to train our eyes to really look, and to register what we have seen in a filing system, and then we need to know how that relates to information we already have.

The trick is not to panic and take in more than you need. Imagine that your brain has a spare folder in its filing cabinet; give it a shape and a colour, and then put in a set of index cards. You now have a special store for observation. When you next need to understand the solution to a problem, for example how the nose joins the face, open up the file to the 'noses' and find the shape you are looking for in your mind's eye. Forget that it's a nose, just think about the shape, otherwise your eyes will wander as they are meant to do, gathering information that you don't need.

Mind you, you do need to exercise some caution, here – staring at people's noses in the street might be seen as threatening behaviour. Try smiling while you do it or wear mirrored sun glasses. If you are doing it on the train or bus, carry a dental tool – no-one will come near you with one of those in your hand. You could even smile, wearing mirrored sun glasses, while playing with a dental tool. Mind you, that might produce a look of fear on some very tight-lipped models! It's better to learn how to glance, look away, register what else you need to know and then glance again. In fact, this will show you what you haven't seen.

It's just a matter of training. I've spent my life in research and continually find the need for new visual information. For instance, I just discovered a new way to work the lips, suggested to me by an actress on television. Don't beat yourself up when you find that you've been doing something wrong. You, too, will see new features everywhere, and remember, you can just try again with a new figure.

Hogarth Hag

23

Body and Head PROPORTIONS

Bob Cratchit and Tiny Tim from Dickens' A Christmas Carol

Music Hall Waiters

I WOULD LOVE TO GET *technical and impress you with my knowledge but to be honest, it's quite simple – just follow the plan. Without a plan of proportions for the human body your figure will not fit comfortably in a room setting and look natural against the furniture. It may only appear to be slightly out, but in miniature even a small amount is magnified; it will look uncomfortable and you will feel frustrated.*

Take a look at different bodies to see how they fit together. Because they do vary so much, do not be tempted to use your own body as a guide for your figure making; I have arms disproportionately long for a man of my height, but I have a theatrical personality and wave them about a lot, so the disproportion does not matter. On a

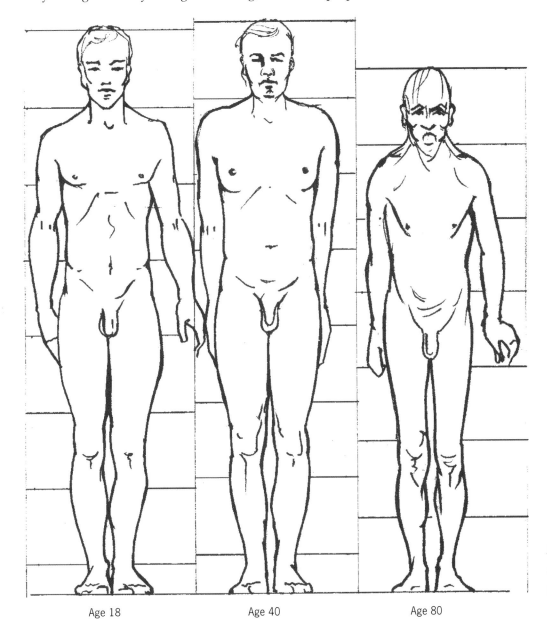

Age 18   Age 40   Age 80

Male proportion chart (reproduced to size)

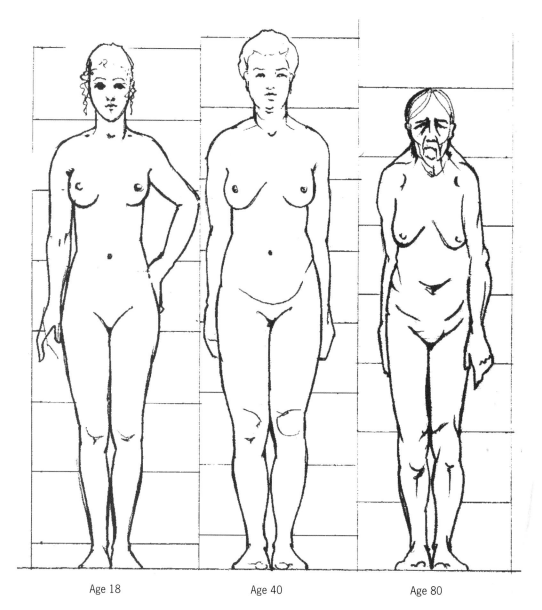

Female proportion chart (reproduced to size)

Age 18   Age 40   Age 80

miniature figure, however, it simply looks odd. Unless there is a good reason to distort the proportions of your figure, they should all follow a basic scheme so that your group of character figures work harmoniously together in a room setting. In this way, no matter how naive your figures, they will always look good.

The proportions for the human form are figured out according to the proportions of the head, and based on the length of the head from the crown to the tip of the chin.

Classic texts on art outline the 'artistic' proportions for the body. In art, there are three different types of proportion for the human form – the heroic, the classic and the romantic. The heroic form stands up to twelve heads high, and applies mainly to the male form; the classic form stands up to nine heads high; and the romantic, again up to twelve heads high, applies to the female form, but the length is concentrated in the leg and is generally associated with fashion. These proportions are unique to

BODY AND HEAD PROPORTIONS

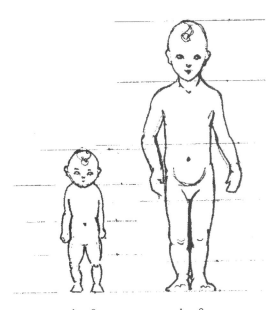

art, and are not appropriate as a guide for the real human form, or for our figures. They are, however, useful for thinking about the different ways in which the human form has been represented.

In this book, I work with adult figures, but I provide a guide to the human form from age 0–80, so that you can see the way the human body changes shape over time. Take a ruler to the heads of each, and you will be surprised by how the human head is already nearly fully formed by the age of two years.

Remember, this scale is for the naked body. Your figure will require dressing too,

Babies and children proportion charts (reproduced to size)

Age 0   Age 2

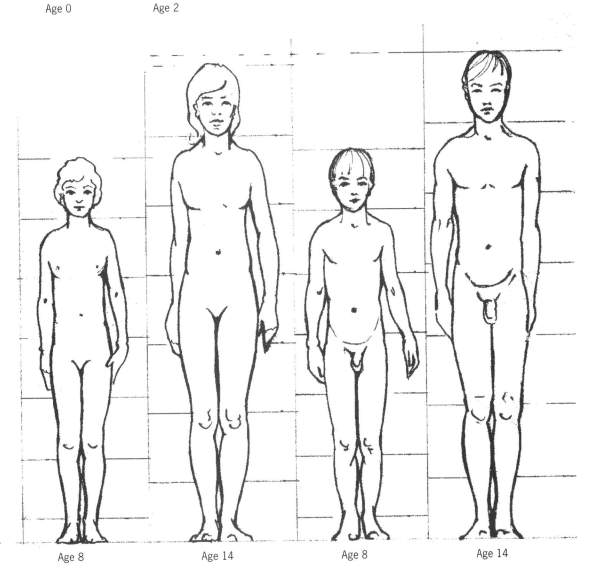

Age 8   Age 14   Age 8   Age 14

and, depending on how much fabric you use, clothing can bulk out your figure, so take this into account as you sculpt the body. Think about how the corset of the period pulls in the body, and where the gathers of a skirt concentrate, or how the collar of a man's shirt and coat will fall, and adjust accordingly. It is better to be on the conservative side, and add more padding later if necessary.

Keep the standard chart to hand as you work, and check it constantly. It is a fact that you only see your mistakes at the very moment you've made that finishing touch to your lovely dressed figure, and oh, the frustration of it!

THE CANON OF THE HUMAN HEAD

For this part of the figure, I'm afraid that we do need to get technical (I can hear your wails from here!). The canon is a system of classification by which the proportions of the head, or body, is understood. All the faces drawn in this book follow this system as a basic guide, represented by a plan. Remember that so-called art teacher who told you that you couldn't draw? Of course you can draw; it was he or she who couldn't teach. Have a go at drawing the canon of the head yourself. You will understand it much better, and you will find that you can draw after all. Following the chart step by step, see how each of the features relates to each other. The message from our eyes to our brain tells us that each feature is a separate unit, but once you know that the width of the nostrils is equal to the width of the space between the eyes, etc., the face starts to look balanced and real, and you can refer back to it at any time if you feel that you have made a mistake along the way. It's much easier to work in this way

instead of trying to estimate how the features fit together. Of course, once you discover that you have the canon right and can draw after all, you can feel really smug, and the next time you are at a gallery with the know-it-all, art critic friend, you can look at a portrait and say knowledgeably: "I think the eyes are sound, but the canon isn't quite right." That's one less Christmas card to send. Like the body, no two faces are the same. Some people have longer chins, plumper cheeks, broader noses and so on, but if you understand the basic canon, you will know the rules that you can then break.

DRAWING THE CANON OF THE HUMAN HEAD

This chart will give you the proportions of the head for adult men and women, young or old.

1 Draw lines across a sheet of paper two and a half units high. Make each unit 1in (25mm), then you can divide it easily.

2 Divide these by two and a half units wide for the front face and three and a half for the profile.

3 Draw a centre line across the two blocks and a centre line down the front face at A. Divide the bottom unit in half at B.

4 Divide the right-hand unit of the front face into two parts to match the other side at C, and a matching line on the other side of the centre line at D.

5 Divide the left-hand unit of the profile into three sections at E and F.

6 Using the illustrations of the canon of the male and female heads, copy the features onto your own grid.

_____

_____

_____

_____

_____

Step 1

Front view   Side view

Step 2

MATERIALS AND EQUIPMENT

A SHEET OF PAPER

RULER

SET SQUARE, OR CORNER OF A PIECE OF CARD

PENCIL

PREPARATION FOR
A BASIC BODY

We are now going to look at the basic male and female torso, aged about thirty years. At this age, the face and body are mature but do not yet show the wear and tear, not to mention the effects of gravity, of age.

31

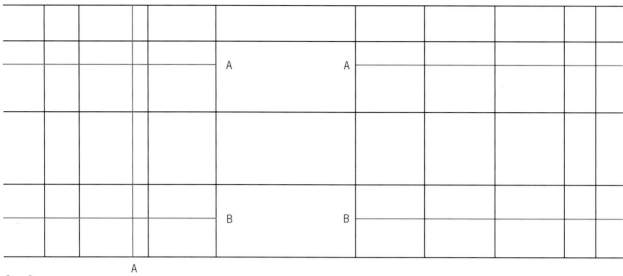

A

Step 3

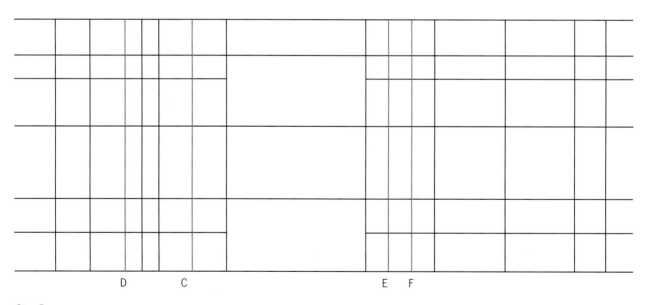

Step 5

Take a look at the common links in the proportion chart for the two sexes. The skeletal and muscular system are similar until puberty, but notice how the shape of each differentiates thereafter. The female (sorry, ladies, but it's a fact) tends to develop a layer of fat over her smaller bone structure, lending her a softer, rounder shape. Her waist is higher and her hips wider than her male counterpart. The male, without this layer of fat, appears more muscular and is more square in shape. As you work, keep in mind that the male is made up of a series of boxes, while the female is a series of spheres.

The faces for each follows much the

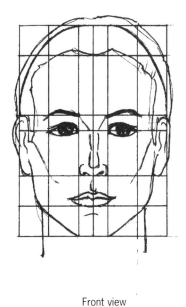

Front view

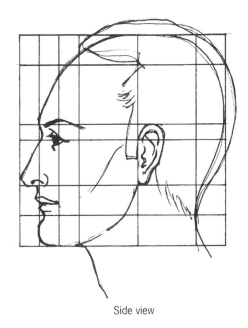

Side view

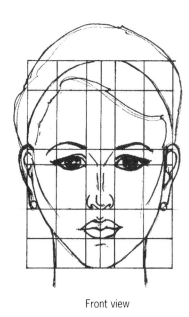

Front view

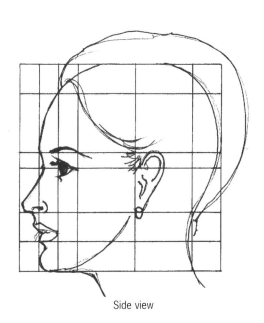

Side view

Step 6. Copying the features onto your own grid

same principle. That of the male tends to be more square, while the female tends to be more round. Of course, we all know women with masculine features and vice versa, but in this instance, we are aiming for standard maculine and feminine faces with regularly proportioned features.

Because we are working in miniature, it is important to emphasize the difference in the sexes by using two different sculpture techniques. On the female, soften any angles on the surface of the clay, and emphasize those on the male.

When you come to work on your figure, switch off one of your light sources. This will send shadows across the plane of the

face or body of your figure. Turn the work in the light so that you can see the angles better. It is this shadow effect that we will be unconsciously aware of when the work is done, and *in situ*. Without shadows we will simply be forming pink blobs, and that's not the effect we want, is it?

BODY SHAPES

Now you understand the proportions of the body, think about how bodies differ. Understanding body shapes enables you to create a figure that looks and stands well. You can't spend time on the face and head without consideration for the body shape; you will not end up with what you want.

Since time began – well, at least, since fashion began – men and women have been uniformly dissatisfied with what Nature has given them, and have tried to pull, push, tighten and pad out to enhance what they have and to look fashionable. Unfortunately, from the moment our ribs are formed our body shape is fixed, and we are stuck with it. The two extremes of body shape are the stocky and the athletic – and most of us fit somewhere in between.

THE STOCKY FIGURE
The stocky figure has a broad, square ribcage with shorter, heavier bones. It is capable of lifting a greater weight than its opposite but the power is short-lived and in bursts of energy. If the stocky figure puts on weight, it becomes larger all over. The silhouette is broad, square, short and robust.

THE ATHLETIC FIGURE
The athletic figure is lean and narrow, like a runner, and is capable of long-term energy

These gentlemen are fine examples of stocky and athletic figures

use. If this figure turns to fat, it collects around the stomach, and it has a tendency to stoop. The ribcage here is very high at the front and centre, curving downwards.

THE CORSET
If your figure is to look correct and of its period, we have to look at the corset. Just when you thought it was all over, here it comes again, back into fashion.

You have only to look at fashion plates of the nineteenth century to see how the corset changes the shape of the human form. Take a look at the illustrations. In the seventeenth century, the breast is compressed by the top of the corset, giving that distinctive 'basket of peaches' look, and the shoulders are fashionably pulled down by their straps. The corset enjoyed lots of change in the nineteenth century. At the beginning, as shown by our illustration of 1810, women must have rejoiced when the fashions freed up their bodies from the restrictions of nipped-in waists, in favour of more flowing dresses which fell from under the bosom. But, before long, trends swung again in favour of the tiny waist, and by the 1880s, the corset extended down to the thighs with the front skirt secured around the back of the legs to hold it smooth to the ankles. So much for freedom of movement. In 1908, the hips are compressed and the breast takes on the appearance of a pouter pigeon. In 1923, the hips are again slim, and the breasts are, for the first time, fashionably small and bound flat.

We can't be too quick to smirk – who amongst us has not tried to get into jeans a little too tight? And don't forget the men. My father, a shoe repairer, had two elderly gentlemen clients, old soldiers, who often brought their corsets in to have them repaired. They were made of linen with pale pink kid edges – never to be forgotten.

The distinctive 'nipped-in' waist

What is a cummerbund, but a corset? And what of 'bombastic' men? Bombast was the padding used in the Tudor period to give men the appearance of a broad chest. It was often their own bed linen.

With the sculpted body, we are more fortunate; you just have to know where the waist fell at any one time and re-sculpt the body. Remember, what gets pulled in must also bulge out somewhere else.

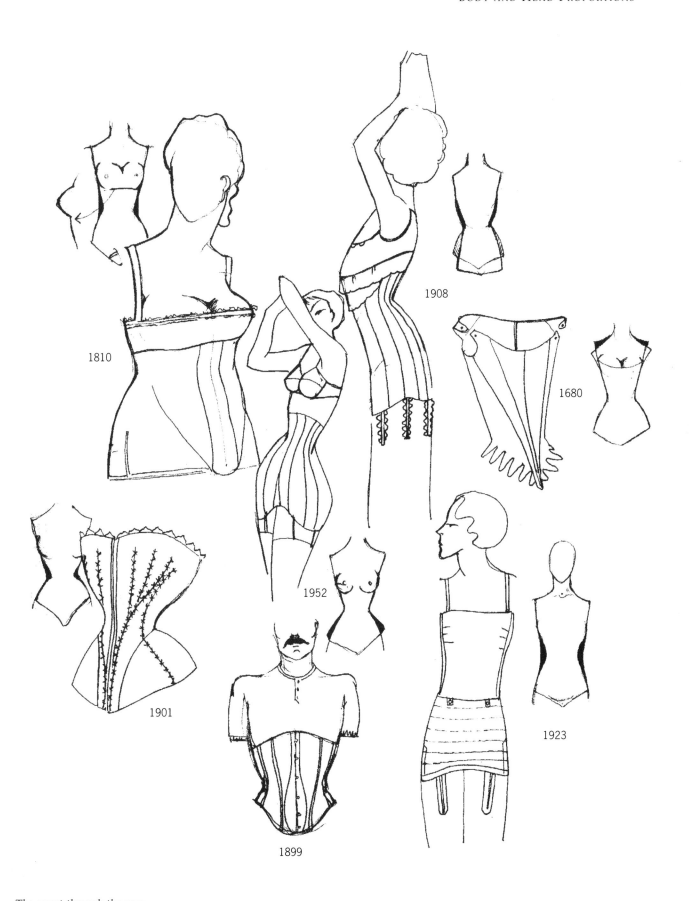

1810

1908

1680

1901

1952

1899

1923

The corset through the ages

Basic Body and HEAD FORMS

Fagin from Dickens' Oliver Twist

The Tarantella

NEXT TIME YOU GO OUT, *take a look at the way people's bodies operate. They are all different. Take one example: a thin, old man. Do other old gentlemen of his age stand and walk in the same way? Some may walk with a stoop, others may have a wide gait. Next time, take a look at a different type. Similarly, see how people carry their heads. Look for weary people as opposed to happy people, both young and old. Look through newspapers for pictures of useful postures and start a scrapbook. But don't overload your mental filing system with too much information; training yourself to find the information you require takes practice.*

BASIC BODY

It is time to get your hands on some clay and create the basic body. The instructions which follow are the same whether you are making a male or female body. Once you have completed one, or better still, one of each, you then have a choice. Use either this method for making *each* figure, or better still, go straight to the next chapter and make a mould. By doing so, you need not do the basic work again – your figures will be proportionally correct no matter whether they are to be eventually thinner, fatter, shorter or taller.

The following method breaks the figure unit into three separate parts: the torso, the head and the neck. This means that you do not have to work the whole of the torso and head in one fell swoop – just take it unit by unit and before long, you will soon get the hang of it.

1 First you need to prepare your work station. Make sure that your work surface is clean and tidy, and lay down some kitchen paper to protect it. Take a clean tile, ready for use. Organize your tools in front of you. Finally, put on an apron, overall or old white shirt and clean your hands.

2 Choose either the male or female torso pattern plan, and either photocopy or trace the outline. Cut out the torso shape, and then transfer this onto a piece of paper or thin card.

3 Make up a block of clay that is to the approximate size of the figure. Work it well in your hands to soften it up. The softer the clay, the better it is to use – half-primed clay can crack in the oven. Get used to doing this now so that you set a precedent for all your future figure work. Once it is softened, block the clay roughly back into shape. You will have more clay than you need so don't worry about getting a perfect shape – you want to get on with it, don't you?

MATERIALS AND EQUIPMENT
·:·

CLAY

KITCHEN PAPER

CLEAN TILE OR OTHER BAKING SHEET

PIN

TOOL 46 OR SCALPEL

MODELLING TOOLS

SOFT ARTIST'S BRUSH

ACETONE

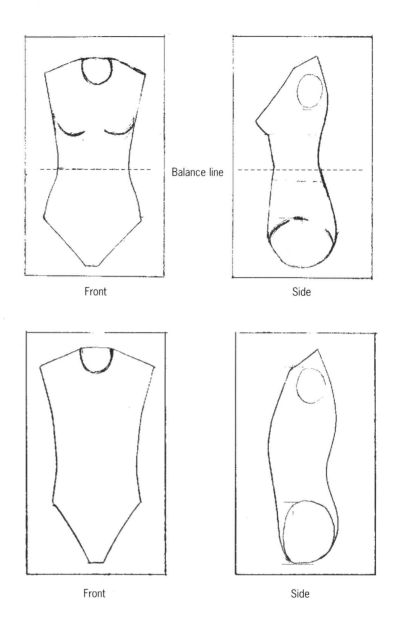

Balance line

Front

Side

Front

Side

*Step 2. Male and
female torso plans
(reproduced to size)*

4 Lay the side plan on the side of the block and prick round the shape to mark the clay. Remove the plan and place the block of clay onto the baking tile. Taking a scalpel or other tool, and keeping it as vertical as you can, cut away the excess clay.

5 As before, place the plan back on the clay and mark the balance line onto it. If you did this at the start, it would probably have disappeared by now.

6 Take the front plan and place it on the front of the torso, matching the balance lines on the side. Try not to let the plan dip into the curves, although remember, it's not brain surgery! Prick around the shape.

7 With the tool or scalpel, cut away the excess as before, but this time do not let the clay rest on a hard surface or you will distort the cut-out shape. Hold it in your hands and trim away a slice at a time. You should have a square-edged shape.

Step 3

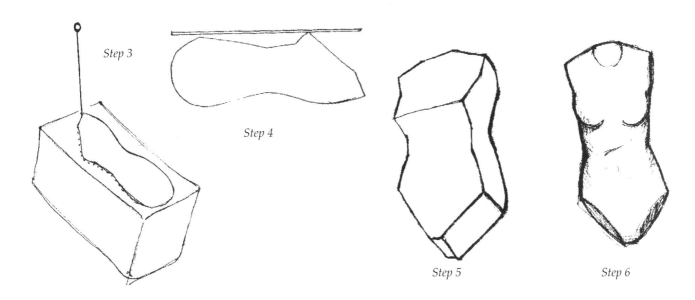

Step 4

Step 5

Step 6

8 You can now do some freehand work – don't be scared. Trim the edges to round off the shape. The best way to trim is to make a cut on one edge and then on the matching side, the same amount. Try doing the right hip, then the left hip first, and then work on the waist. Don't try to do too much with one cut – you can always add some clay later if necessary. As you work, get used to looking at your work from every angle to ensure that the form of your figure is well-balanced.

9 When you are happy with your work (are we ever..?), take a metal tool and lightly smooth over the clay. It doesn't have to be perfect at this stage; you can finish it properly after the clay has a chance to rest and firm up. While it does this, you have time to get on with the other parts – the figure's head and neck.

BASIC HEAD AND NECK

Now we arrive at what is, for many, the most daunting bit – the head. But don't fear, remember we are focusing on the proportions and not the features of the basic shape. The amount of clay you need has been worked out for you, so there's no excuse; proceed with confidence.

Working the torso

Step 2. The head block (reproduced approximately to size)

Forming the head

Step 3

Step 4

Step 5

Step 6

1 Start as you did before; clean your hands, prepare your work surface and put on an apron, ready to begin.

2 Make up a block of clay to the size shown (page 43). This means forming it exactly to size for the female head and to just (and I mean just) outside the line for the male head. It's only a marginal difference, but it is important. In reality, a man's head is sometimes smaller than that of a woman, but for this exercise we will keep to what looks better. We will work on differences later when we add the features.

3 Roll the block into an egg shape, and flatten the base at an angle.

4 Pinch in the cheeks, applying equal pressure to each side.

5 Check it all round to ensure that you have a balanced shape.

6 Flatten the mouth area slightly from under the nose to the tip of the chin, and square it off. The main aim of this process is to get the planes of the face established, so that you have a reference to work with.

7 Using the canon as a guide, mark in the centre line down the face and then the halfway line to see where the eyes will fall. You don't need to do any more than that. The rule, if there is one, is to keep it simple.

8 Now create the neck. At this stage, the neck appears to be just a tube of clay, but keep in mind a mental image of the bones and muscles inside the neck which support the head, allowing it to twist and turn. It also contains the voice-box which allows us to speak, and the gullet, which allows us to swallow. So, it's quite vital really. But let's keep it simple. Make up the tube to the thickness shown, and pinch the front edge slightly so that it looks a little bit egg-shaped when viewed from above.

9 Carefully cut the length off at the angles shown. If it becomes a little lopsided, reshape it. The angles will set the neck at a slight angle on the torso and support the head slightly ahead of the chest. If you need to check the angle you require, use your own head as a guide. If you use a hand mirror to look into a larger mirror, you will be able to see the angle you are aiming for.

ASSEMBLY

1 Take the torso and flatten off the area where the neck will sit. Scratch some lines into the clay on the torso and neck end to help you bond the two parts together properly. Place in position and, using the wooden tool, blend in the join. Do the same to the head and to the top of the neck. You now have a proportionally correct character figure blank.

2 If you feel happy with the result and you are going to make a mould of it, give the whole thing a wash with acetone using the soft brush. This will remove any scratches and fingerprints, but at the same time will also make the clay impossible to work on any further, so be warned.

Step 8. The neck tube (reproduced approximately to size)

Step 9. Cutting the angle

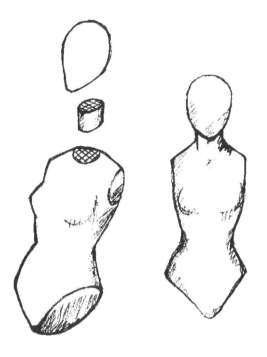

Step 1. Assembling the torso

THE SEATED FIGURE

To add variety to a group of figures, it is often pleasing to have one or two of them sitting down. One thing that drives me mad is a figure wobbling on a chair with its feet dangling into space. Basically, a figure made to stand will never sit properly. Make your seated figures in a seated position from the start. Please note that upholstered chairs will be higher than standard ones and the figure will not weigh enough to depress the cushion as it would in real life. To remedy this, either remove the cushion if it is a separate unit, slit the fabric of the cushion and remove the padding, or if it's not, sew the padding down through the base of the seat.

1 Model the torso as for a standing figure, then chop off the crotch area and add on some extra clay to square off the bottom of the torso.

2 Seat the figure on a chair, twisting the body until it looks comfortable.

3 Flatten off the front of the pelvis, and make holes to accommodate lengths of wire to be inserted later.

4 When making up, keep trying the figure on the chair. You may need to exaggerate the length of the leg to get a well-balanced figure, so don't be too hasty to glue before you do a fitting.

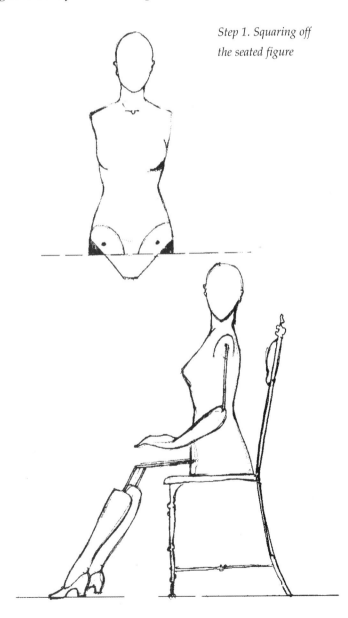

Step 1. Squaring off the seated figure

Step 2. Fitting the seated figure

45

Making a
MOULD

The Tango

T*HIS IS THE PROCESS I find most difficult to approach. I think it's because I can hear my mother from childhood, wailing about getting the kitchen in a mess, when in fact it was my elder sister who spilled all the plaster – and I got the blame! However, it's an important job and once complete, I get a real thrill from it. It also cuts out an enormous amount of preparation work; I can start a new figure without having to go through this first stage each time.*

Before we start, let me make one plea – find a plastic bucket and fill it with water. I know you are going to follow all my instructions implicitly, but I guarantee this will be the one you forget until it's too late. The reason? No plaster must get into the sink – whether it be powder, liquid or set plaster – it will bung up the downpipe like magic, and we all know plumber's fees are astronomical!

MAKING A MOULD WITH WALLS

1 Take a plastic bucket and fill it up with water.

2 Make up a block of modelling clay or Plasticine ¾in (20mm) larger than the figure and about 1in (25mm) in depth, and place this on a tile or another work surface.

MATERIALS AND EQUIPMENT

———— ❖ ————

TOOL NO. 46 OR SCALPEL

TILE OR OTHER FLAT BASE

ROLLING PIN OR GLASS BOTTLE

SURFORM, RASP OR COARSE SANDPAPER

PARTING AGENT

MODELLING CLAY OR PLASTICINE

(TWO LARGE PACKS)

MIXING POT, RUBBER BOWL OR EMPTY

MARGARINE TUB

PLASTER (PREFERABLY KAFFIR 'D', AVAILABLE

FROM DENTAL SUPPLIERS)

SOFT TOOTHBRUSH OR HOG-HAIR BRUSH

SURGICAL GLOVES OR BARRIER CREAM

(FOR SENSITIVE SKIN)

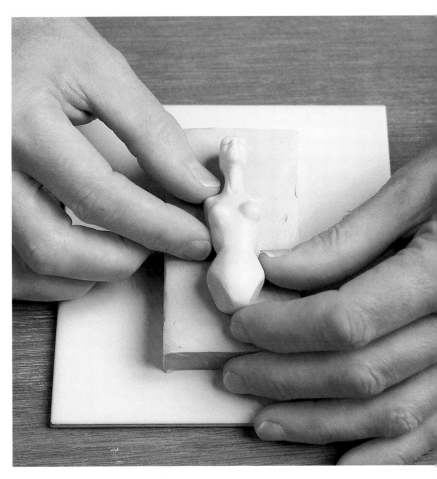

Step 2. Placing the figure on a tile

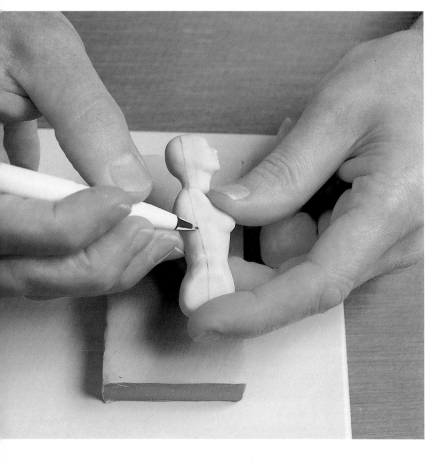

3 Mark the halfway point around the figure. Check that there are no undercuts that will get trapped in the mould, under the chin, for example. These can be filled in with a little clay. Don't worry, they can be trimmed off the finished figure later.

4 Place the figure face up on the clay bed and prick out the outline with tool 46, a long pin or a scalpel. Keep the tool vertical as you work. Remove the figure to leave the plan in the bed.

5 Cut out a pit in the bed of clay to take the figure.

6 Fit the figure in the pit and check the halfway mark. Adjust until you are happy, and fill in any gaps. It is important that you try to keep the bed clay as flat as possible as you do so.

Step 3. Marking the halfway point

Step 4. Pricking out the outline

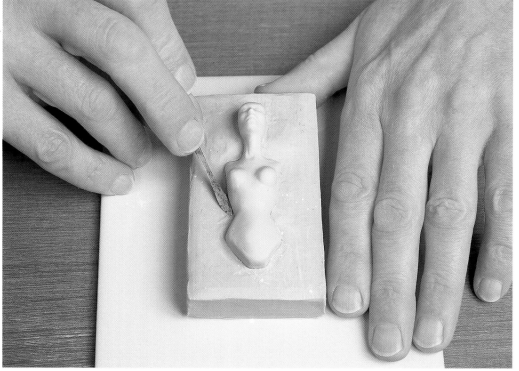

*Step 5. Cutting out
a pit in the clay*

*Step 6. Fitting the
figure in the pit*

7 Make the holes for keying the moulds together. Stick in the end of a pencil and wiggle it around, not too deeply, until you get a smooth, funnel shape.

8 Make the walls a good ½in (12mm) thick. Be quite generous because they need to contain the liquid plaster. The plaster appears to have a thick consistency when you pour it, but any weakness in the walls and the plaster will escape faster than a child leaving school, and there is very little you can do to stop it. Before you know it, you've lost a quarter of a pint and you can guarantee that the only thing to hand will be those new tea towels. Be warned, I've done it.

Step 7. Making holes to key the moulds

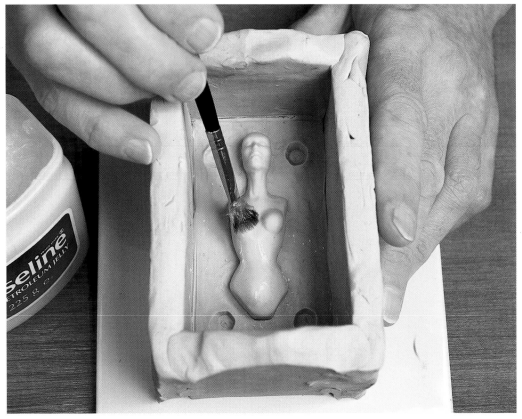

Step 11. Preparing the figure for the mould

9 Taking the clay or Plasticine, make more fat rolls for the walls than you think you will need, and roll them flat with a rolling pin or, for the hygienically minded, a glass bottle. Trim the long sides square. They will need to be about 1in (25mm) higher than the highest point of your figure.

10 Cut them to length and fit around the bed clay, pressing the joins firmly.

11 To prepare the figure for the mould, take some petroleum jelly, silicon spray or cooking oil, and carefully coat the figure. This will help to release the figure from the plaster. Forget this now and you will be in big trouble later.

MIXING THE PLASTER

1 Open the tub of plaster and put it in a safe place, not on the draining board, but near the bucket. (Repeat after me: 'Blocked drain…plumber's bill…blocked drain…plumber's bill…'.) If you have used modelling clay you will have to guess how much water you need, but with Plasticine, you can fill the mould with water to just slightly more than halfway and tip this into your mixing container.

2 If you have sensitive skin, put on thin surgical gloves or barrier cream now.

3 It's not a good idea to hold the water-filled pot over the plaster in case you drop it, but I think we all do, so take a firm grip, sprinkle the plaster over the water until peaks form on the surface which do not sink when you shake the pot.

4 This is the last call for that bucket of water I keep going on about!

5 Push the back of your fingers into the pot and gently swirl and scoop the plaster mixture, creating as few air bubbles as possible, until you have a smooth mixture. If the consistency is too thin, use

Step 5. Mixing the plaster

Step 6. Rinsing off in the bucket

the hand which is not wet to sprinkle a little more plaster into the mixture, and then mix a second time.

6 Rinse your fingers thoroughly in the bucket of water.

7 Bang the pot onto a hard surface to release any trapped air bubbles in the mixture, then pour into the mould. Start pouring into the corner of the mould and let the plaster seep around the figure. I've watched my dentist make his moulds and he stops pouring when the plaster just covers the object, then takes a paintbrush and brushes the plaster into any details that may have air trapped in them. I recommend that you try this, but wash the brush immediately. Continue pouring until the mould is full.

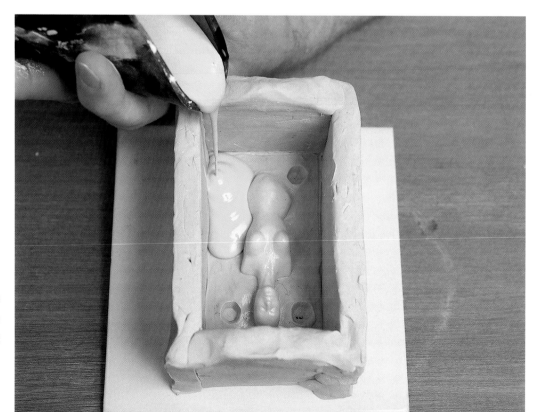

Step 7. Pouring the plaster mixture into the mould

8 To dispel any final air bubbles, lift the corner of the base tile a little and let it bang down, and repeat until you think they have dispelled. (A quick prayer that the walls hold will not be amiss.)

9 Leave to cure. This means that as soon as the water makes contact with the plaster, the plaster becomes active and turns into a chain, like a whole host of worms that link up and solidify. At its most active, it heats up; leave it to cool, and you can make the other half of the mould.

MAKING THE OTHER HALF OF THE MOULD

1 Peel away the walls and the base clay and clean the surface with a tool. Don't go mad, just a little will do.

Step 8. Banging the mould onto a work surface to dispel air bubbles

Step 1. Peeling away the walls and base clay

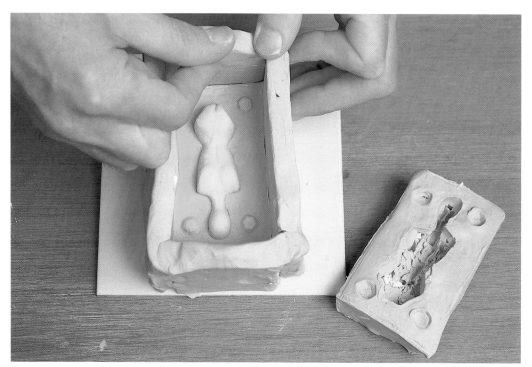

Step 3. Rebuilding the clay walls for the second half of the mould

Step 1. Peeling off the walls for the second time

2 Coat the surface, figure and plaster with your releasing agent, avoiding the sides. (Now say – "I have coated the surface with my chosen releasing agent!") There is nothing worse than parting a mould that insists on doing the opposite.

3 Rebuild the walls in the same way as you did before.

4 Mix and pour in the plaster, as you did before for the first half.

5 Dispel any air bubbles by banging the pot on a hard work surface again.

6 Set the mould aside until the plaster is cold after it has cured.

FINISHING

1 Peel away the walls and, if you've used modelling clay rather than Plasticine, clean it up, spray it with water, and seal in a bag for later use.

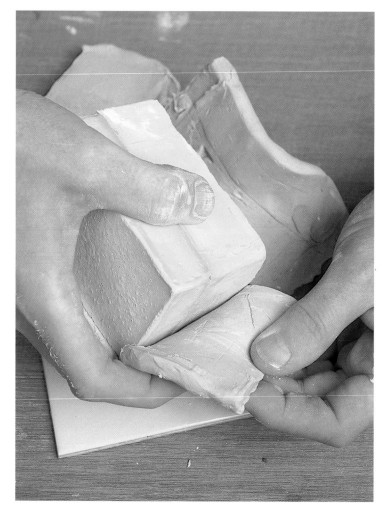

*Step 2. Softening
the edges of the clay*

*Step 3. Removing
the figure*

2 Take your Surform, rasp or sandpaper
and clean up the outside of the mould,
smoothing off all the edges so that you have
a comfortable grip. It is best to do this
immediately, before the plaster becomes too
hard to work off.

3 Prise the two halves apart. This can be
an agonizing moment, but if you've
followed the instructions it should come
apart – even if you have to resort to tapping
a screwdriver into the join. (Yes, I've had
occasion to do this before.)

4 Clean the mould in warm water and
washing-up liquid using a soft
toothbrush or hog-hair brush. It is almost
impossible to do this completely, but with
time and usage, it will clean.

5 It is best to put the two halves together
and leave for 24 hours. If like me you
do not have the patience of a saint, take a
pull now. This may distort the mould a little
but it doesn't pose too much of a problem.

CLEANING UP

1 Wash everything *in the bucket* and leave it to settle. After an hour all the plaster will have sunk to the bottom and set. (Imagine that going down the sink.)

2 Pour off the water somewhere safe and dispose of the set plaster in the bin.

MAKING A MOULD WITH BRICK WALLS

This is not a course in brickbuilding, but a way of making walls for your mould using children's plastic building bricks, like Lego. (To stop your irate family and friends from writing me letters, I would ask that you buy a box of your own.)

1 To embed the figure in the clay, follow the same method, but when you make up the initial block, surround it with a layer of bricks. Once the figure is in the bed, rather than make clay walls, simply build up the bricks to the height you require. Any gaps between the clay and the bricks can easily be filled in with extra clay. This method gives you a really neat, square-sided, finished mould. You need only round off its edges a little to give it a good, comfortable grip.

2 There are bound to be small gaps between the bricks, but for some reason the plaster doesn't seem to leak through them too much. As an added safeguard, run some masking tape around the walls before you pour the plaster in. (Another reason to buy your own bricks – yes, I know you think that you'll wash any plaster off, but...)

3 When you've made the first half of the mould, simply turn it over, walls and

all. Peel off the bedding clay, paint on the parting agent and pour in the second layer of plaster. If you need deeper walls, just add on a couple more brick layers.

4 You may need to prise the first brick off with the tip of a knife, but they do come away quite easily.

TAKING A PULL

I know this may sound rather rude, but it simply means making a solid cast from your mould.

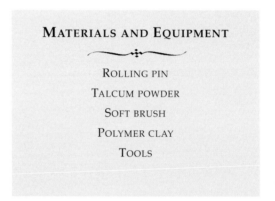

MATERIALS AND EQUIPMENT

ROLLING PIN

TALCUM POWDER

SOFT BRUSH

POLYMER CLAY

TOOLS

Step 3. Pressing clay into the mould

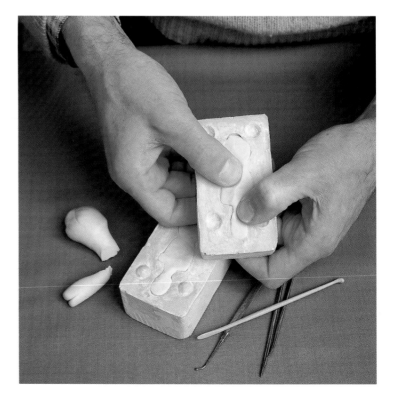

1 To allow the clay to release easily from the mould, dust the inside with talcum powder. Tip a small pile onto a saucer, pick some up with a soft brush and dust over the surface. Blow off the excess. (If you wear glasses, it is a good idea to clean them now.) After you have used the mould a few times, check to see that there is no build-up of powder in the details of the face. If there is, wash the mould.

2 Estimate how much clay you need and soften it really well in your hands.

3 Take enough clay to fill half the mould and press in well, leaving a fraction above the mould, then fill the other half.

4 Roughen up the surface of both halves in a criss-cross motion to key the parts to be joined.

5 Press the two parts together, working from side to side and corner to corner.

Step 4. Roughening the surface

Step 5. Pressing the mould joins together

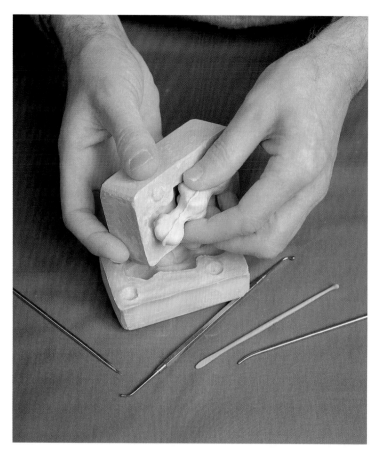

6 Pull the mould apart and gently ease out the figure.

7 Clean off the joins. If there are any small gaps where the two halves have pulled away from each other, work the edges together.

8 If there were any air bubbles trapped in the mould, they will now appear on the figure. You can guarantee that they will be on the inside of one eye in a difficult part to reach. Don't worry, just work them off and generally clean the face ready for its facial expression.

9 If the first pull does not come out clean, you can use this first figure as a practice model.

Step 6. Easing out the figure

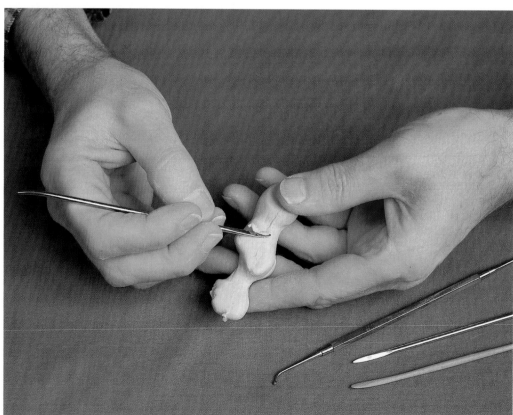

Step 7. Cleaning off the joins

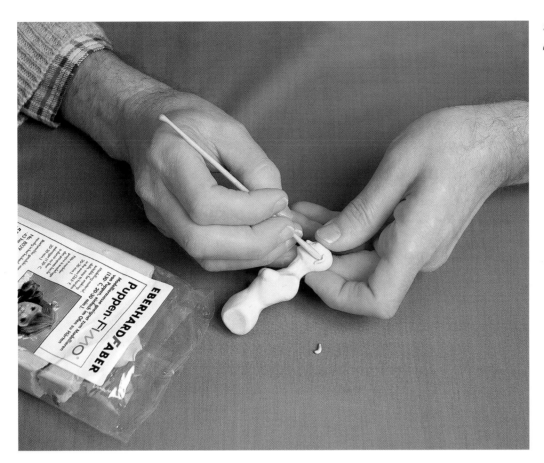

*Step 10. Adding the
ears to the figure*

10 Add the ears now. It is important to
do this first so that you have a
guide for the cheekbone and jaw line. Make
two small pieces of clay into the shape of
orange segments and, checking the canon
to see where they fit, place them on either
side of the head. View the head from the
front and the top to check that they are
level. Press them onto the head with a
wooden tool and smooth out, giving the
impression of an ear.

11 Complete the rest of the figure's
features to your requirements.

12 Make holes in the shoulders and
bottom of the torso so you will be
able to that you can join the wires later.

*Step 12. Making
holes for the wires*

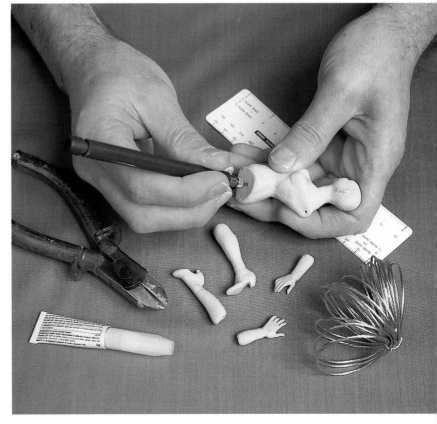

Skull and
FACE SHAPES

The Country Wife

To UNDERSTAND THE HUMAN SKULL *is also to understand what happens to the face and its features. Many books on anatomy give you a list of the names of bones, but, with due respect, often appear to be written with brain surgeons rather than artists in mind. Latin names can be daunting and confuse the issue.*

Simply, the skull is made up of two parts: the cranium, which is the top part, and the lower maxillary, which is the jawbone and chin. The jawbone is the only moveable part, allowing us to talk, laugh, eat, cry, etc. The hinge is set at just below the ears. The important thing to remember is that when the jaw opens, rather than drop straight downwards, the hinge operates and the chin moves down towards the throat. If the throat is fleshy, the skin will squash up and gather into rolls, and this is called the chin strap. Some lucky people have clean jaw lines, to the extent that they often form a hollow under the jawbone instead. One consolation is that they often look scrawny in old age (at least, I always hope so).

The shape of the skull influences the shape of the face; it's the only part of the skeleton to do this. Consulting the line drawings, right, look at the black outlines around the skull, at the jawbone, cheekbones, forehead and scalp. The muscles and tissue are not very bulky, so the outline of the skull is very pronounced, which shows how the shape of the skull determines the shape of the head. Even on a fat face, the skull influences the shape. Think of it this way. Imagine that you have a wet cloth draped over a football. If you gather the cloth tightly under the ball, it approximates the way flesh clings to the bones of a young, muscular face. Gather it more loosely, and it will drape at the base but still cling to the

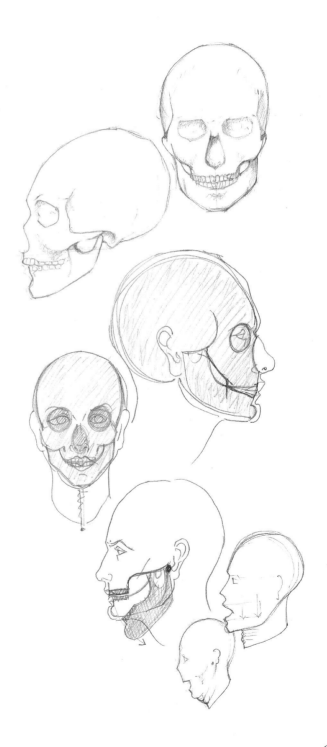

The composition and workings of the skull

The male and female faces, top, fit the standard canon and the pair, bottom, extend beyond it

upper part. Place a couple of potatoes inside the wet cloth and you will see how they weigh the cloth downwards, like fat on a full face, but the top part of the skull is still well-defined. Fat does not develop outwards; that wretched thing called gravity (as some of us know, to our cost) pulls the face downwards, and with it, features like the eyes and mouth.

If you are a 'certain age', and feel very brave, test this theory by placing a mirror flat on a table, and lean over it to look at yourself. (Remove all sharp objects out of the way before you do this!) The effect can be devastating, and you may find yourself not daring even to glance down in public

These characters are fine examples of different skull and face shapes

for the rest of your life. Of course, if you are young, this will not happen – well, not today perhaps, but it will, so work on your sense of humour now; you'll need it!

Redraw, or trace, the faces and their profiles from the canon and try to fit the skull onto these. Keep them to hand when you come to sculpt the faces. Practise with these, and you will pick up some valuable information about the relationship between the face and skull as you progress.

The skull of the male and female are identical in structure, but the female's is slightly lighter and rounder at the top of the eye bone and at the jaw. In comparison, the male has a ridge running over the eyebrows which can be quite pronounced, to the point where it produces a shadow across the eyes in the manner of Mr Rochester or Mr Darcy. If the face also has a pronounced cheekbone, the effect is very masculine (a fact which is quite hard for those of us with faces as angular as a boiled egg!). On a female face, strong cheekbones give the face a classic beauty. Indeed, models in the fifties used to have their back teeth removed to emphasize this shape, but if too pronounced, they can make the face seem a little hard.

Close your eyes, and use your fingers to feel around your eye sockets and the join between the sockets and the cheekbones. Register the relationship between these shapes in your mind. Now pick up a small mirror and look through this into a larger mirror to see your face at different angles, observing how the planes of the face relate around the eyes.

EXERCISE

Go out and look at people in the street. Look at faces with prominent cheekbones, and those with rather less pronounced ones, too. See how the brow bones affect the look of a person, and the jawbone, too. If you follow this feature by feature, and don't try to take in too much at once, pretty soon you will train yourself to observe the whole face without a problem, and you will be able to look for a specific type of face with ease.

FACE SHAPES

As we have seen, the bones of the skull affect the shape of the face. There are four basic face shapes: square, heart-shaped, oval and round. The shape is dictated by the lower half of the face because the dome remains virtually the same for each. It is worth noting here that the shape of one's face is an indication of the shape and form of the whole skeletal structure. There are no hard and fast rules, but generally, thin faces have thinner bodies and vice versa.

SQUARE

A square-shaped face is more masculine, and the one most men would prefer to have (me, to name one). The jawbone is almost level until it rises sharply upwards towards the ear, and can, in extreme cases, also point outwards. Most commonly, a square jaw is coupled with taut skin and sharply defined cheekbones causing a hollow to form in the cheeks themselves. The skin then stretches around the teeth and can result in a 'canine' jaw. Fat on the face will often produce a wide neck line.

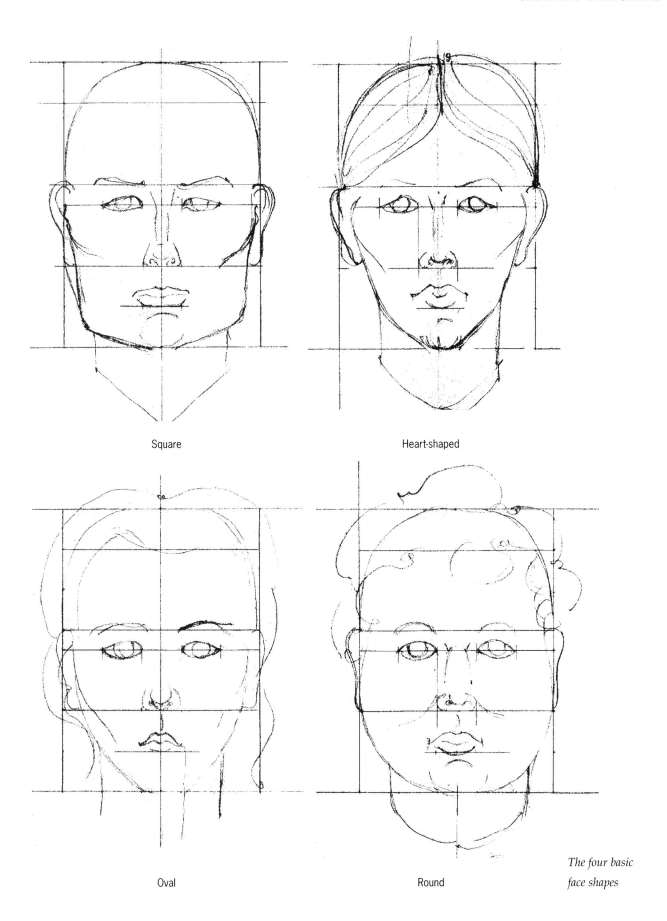

Square

Heart-shaped

Oval

Round

*The four basic
face shapes*

69

HEART-SHAPED

The heart-shaped face is the opposite of a square one, and generally considered to be the most feminine. Although the width of the skull at ear level remains much the same, the softly angled jaw line can produce the effect of width at the temples. The jaw rises upwards from the chin at a sharp angle to the ears, sometimes at two points, which gives the jaw an angular shape. The chin looks small and pointed and high cheekbones emphasize the width of the face. Generally, fat gathers at the throat, sagging at the side of the mouth and either side of the chin.

OVAL

The sides of the face are almost vertical for this face shape, and the jaw line is evenly curved with no angles. The face has gently rounded bones with little prominence, and the features are pleasantly proportioned. Any fat on the face is distributed evenly and emphasizes the oval shape of the face even further.

ROUND

The round face is like the oval, but wider across the face, a result of the flat, broad cheekbones which tend to jut outwards rather than forwards. The jaw line follows that of the square-shaped face, but without the angles. The bones of the skull for a round face are generally heavier and flatter, and the facial features also tend to be rounder than on other face shapes. Fat on the face hangs from the broad cheekbones and makes the neck appear to be very wide, and the chin small and pronounced.

EXERCISE

As you go about your daily business, look for the four basic face shapes on people of a range of ages over a four-day period, one shape at a time.

ALTERING THE SHAPE WITHIN THE CANON

Now that you are familiar with the basic face shapes, it's time to break the rules, such as they are. We all know faces that do not fit comfortably inside the canon, and it would be very boring if they did.

Look at the illustrations of different face shapes. The first face (A) represents 'Mr Normal'. Although he is gaining in age, the flesh on his face is still reasonably firm and stays within the confines of the grid, but look at what happens to him as the facial tissue loses its elasticity in the last face (D); the jaw line drags quite a bit below the canon line. The second face (B) has a chin which is longer than the standard. The third face (C) falls short of the standard.

Take a pencil and try drawing them in profile to see what other distortions become apparent. You could give the second face (B) a much more pronounced or receding lower jaw – which ones looks stubborn, and which one weak? Perhaps on the third face (C), you could experiment with the profile of the nose. If you choose to make it flat and tip-tilted, you will produce a face that does not age, but what happens if you curse it with a nose a Gladiator would be proud of? Take off the chin, too, and what do you get? Have fun with these faces, but beware of making them caricatures; it's fine as an exercise, but not for a natural-looking figure.

A

B

C

D

*Different face
shapes and their
relationship to
the canon*

Basic
FEATURES

The Scarlet Madam

*W*HETHER YOU HAVE MOULDED *or made your basic body, you are now ready to work the basic facial features. Male or female, it doesn't matter; the features may be different, but the principle is the same.*

To begin with, it is preferable to work the foundations of the facial features and then once you are satisfied with the balance, go back over them to work the detail.

1 Make sure that the canon lines are still clear on the face, and lightly mark out the spacing for the eyes.

2 Take one of the ball-ended tools and make hollows for the eye sockets – not too deep, though, you're not drilling for oil.

3 Roll out a tiny length of clay and cut it into two equal parts to make the eye dome which takes up the upper and lower lid and the eyeball. Roll the two lengths into balls and squash them into flattish shapes. Now make two more, since it's likely that one of them has now disappeared forever.

4 Put each one carefully into place and, using a wooden tool, smooth the edges out. It's maddening the way they sometimes stick to the tool rather than the head, but they eventually comply.

TIP

Handle the figure very lightly. The temptation is to be unaware of how tense the hands can become as you work. Stop every so often, put the work down and massage your fingers; this will help to keep them relaxed. When working from this book, try propping it open in front of you, and set aside enough time to follow the instructions in a relaxed manner. This is not a project you can do in a hurry.

5 Using your tool, mark the line for the mouth and an equal amount on either side for the width.

6 Mark the width of the nostrils at the point where the nose joins the upper lip.

MATERIALS AND EQUIPMENT

CLAY

CLEAN WORK SURFACE

TOOLS

ACETONE

SOFT ARTIST'S BRUSH

PENCIL

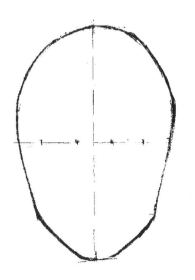

Working the facial features

Step 1

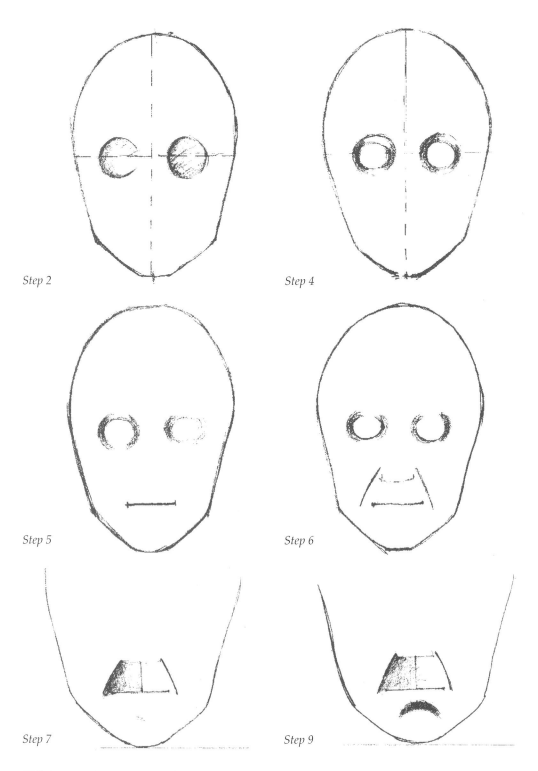

Step 2

Step 4

Step 5

Step 6

Step 7

Step 9

7 Cut two lines running from the edge of the nostrils to around the outside of the mouth. This defines the cheek area.

8 Take the edge of one of the metal tools and drag a small amount of clay from this edge to the centre of the upper lip.

Repeat this on the other side so that you make a rounded shape with a slight peak where they meet. Think about the structure underneath the top lip. The temptation is to make this part flat, and it's not. To see what I mean, run your tongue over your top teeth and feel the curve.

9 Take the ball tool and work the chin in what appears to be an upside-down U shape. This will, at the same time, start to form the lower lip. When we think about the shape of lips, we tend to think in terms of their colour and, because of this, assume that they have a sharp outline. In fact, the lower lip is rather like a sausage, with little sections of fat running downwards at each side of the mouth.

10 Now do the nose. Make a long, triangular shape out of the clay to fit the area of the nose and place in position, then use the wooden tool to blend.

11 The basic features should now be in place. Check that they look balanced, but do not be tempted to overwork them. Let the piece rest for a few minutes to give the clay time to firm up, ready for the next stage. Now we come to refining the features.

EYES

1 Following the curve of the eyeball, cut a shallow line at the upper eyelash.

2 Scrape downwards a very thin layer of clay to reveal the eyeball, then smooth out the spare clay down towards the cheekbone.

3 Define the lower line of the eye with a thin cut.

4 Take the pointed end of the tool and clean up the inner and outer points of the eyeball. Mark in the crease between the bone above the eye and the upper eyelid. As you work, remember that the eyeball is just that – a ball set into a socket.

5 The final cleaning up can be done later with some acetone.

Creating the eyes

TIP

It may seem the most natural thing in the world, but during the next part it's a good idea to remember to breathe.

When you get to the really fine details, notice how tempting it is not to do so. Your whole body becomes tense, your shoulders end up around your ears and your hands stiffen up. Stop, drop your shoulders down and massage your fingers, and breathe until you start work again. Don't you feel better?

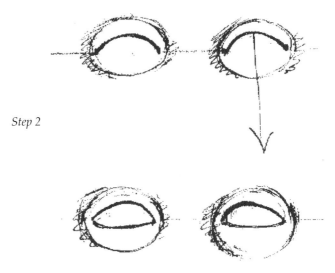

Step 2

Step 3

Step 4

LIPS

1 Using the tool as a knife, score a gently curving line to mark the join between the lips.

2 Using the flat side of the same tool, smooth the clay upwards to create the upper lip.

3 Take the flat of the tool again and smooth downwards from the nostril area to the edge of the lip to create a slight ridge. Work upwards and downwards with the tool, and repeat until you are satisfied with the result.

4 Now smooth down the lower lip, remembering that quite often the outer edge of this lip forms a roll. If you prefer fuller lips, add tiny rolls of clay to fill them out and smooth them onto the main body of the face.

5 Check the profile of the lips, ensuring they are natural-looking.

6 Try to sculpt the upper lip so that it protrudes slightly in front of the lower. Don't do too much or you will produce a buck-toothed look, and not too little or it will look sulky. (No mistake is wasted, however – just remember what the mistake looks like for future reference.)

7 Take the ball tool and press it into the corner of the mouth, which makes the lower lip appear to protrude from beneath the upper one. Notice how this simple hollow can change the whole facial expression, and file it away in your mental filing system.

NOSE

1 Make a triangular nose shape from the clay and place into position. Take the ball tool and, keeping a careful check on the profile of the face, smooth out the edges of the face.

2 Run the ball tool around the tip of the nose, and make a slight indent above the nostrils.

Working the lips

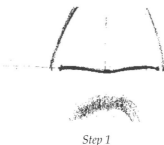

Step 1

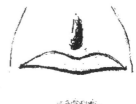

Step 3

Step 4

3 Cut a fine line around the outer nostril, and with the pointed tool, clean up around the area.

4 With the pointed tool, make the nostrils and run a line down the centre of the upper lip.

JAW LINE, NECK AND SHOULDERS

Use the ball tool to define the jaw line, and mark the long downward hollows on the neck and shoulder areas.

EARS

This is a good time to place the ears on the figure if you do not do it when you are working the basic body. The ears fall on the mould line and can be very fiddly but they always work out fine (see page 61 for full instructions).

FINISHING

If you are going to make a mould at this stage, and I highly recommend that you do, simply wash the whole thing with acetone to remove any scratches and fingerprints. If you think you need to work any further modelling, use a very fine brush. Don't worry if some of the edges blur; even though you have now rendered the clay useless for modelling, you can redefine the edges carefully with one of the metal tools. Don't overwork your work!

Sculpting the nose

Step 1

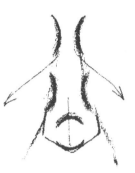

Step 2

Step 3

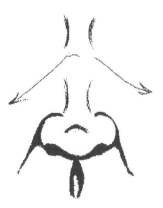

Step 4

Hands and FEET

Playtime With Papa

HANDS

Some years ago I decided to make larger dolls than those featured in this book, but was worried about doing the hands. I was struck by a plan to off-load the problem onto a brilliant sculptress friend of mine. I phoned her and asked her to do them for me. She refused. I whined that I couldn't do them and that I needed her help. She was quick to point out my problem. It wasn't that I couldn't do the hands, she said; the stumbling block was the fear of doing the second hand. Feeling ticked off and in a slight temper, I decided to prove her wrong – and I have been making pairs of hands ever since.

Without a nice pair of hands, your figure will be just another doll. Hands are like punctuation marks in a well-composed sentence; they emphasize the expression and, even in repose, add the final touch to the mood and emotion of the figure.

Practise, practise, practise and, like most things that are worth learning, it will pay off in spades.

It is tempting to leave the hands until later when you have a set of bodies, and this may suit the masochists amongst us, but it's not worth it. Work the hands at the same time as the body so that they match. I argue with myself that doing ten pairs of hands works better, that I will 'get into the swing' of making them, but it doesn't work that way. I spend way too much time projecting on the never-ending sets of hands ahead, and lose my sense of concentration on the pair I'm working on at the time.

In fact, there are no standard hands, only a basic shape. Hands are much larger than you think (mine in particular), but unless the figure requires them, they don't have to be coarse. Remember, too,

MATERIALS AND EQUIPMENT

CLAY

CLEAN WORK SURFACE

TOOLS

SCISSORS

that the hand is about the length of the distance between the chin to the forehead.

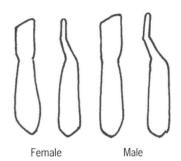

Guides for hands

Female   Male

1 Work the clay really well in your hands until it is smooth and soft. This is very important because it gives the clay the flexibility it needs to endure the amount of handling. For this reason, make one hand at a time.

2 Make up the basic hand shape, taking care that the hand part is as near to the illustration, above, as possible. Don't worry about the wrist and forearm at this stage, we will deal with that later.

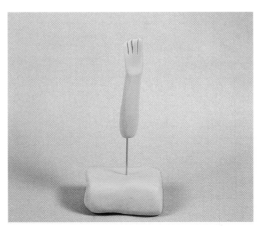

Creating the hands

Step 3

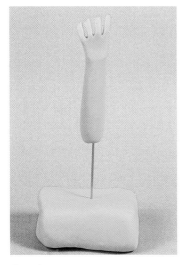

Step 4

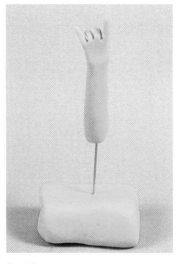

Step 5

Step 6

Step 7

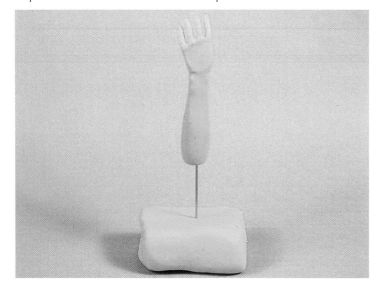

Step 8

3 Take a pair of small, pointed scissors and cut the hand into fingers. Try not to let the scissors close together completely at the end; this can sometimes cause fractures across the base which weakens the whole hand.

4 Take the wooden tool and separate the fingers – gently does it.

5 Bend down all but one finger and pinch the tip with your fingers to round off the end of each. Fold this one down and gently raise the next one. Repeat. (Now you can see why the clay has to be well worked!)

6 Take the pointed metal tool and lay the point on each finger to mark the cuticle base, then scribe a line each side of the nail.

7 Each finger will have a sharp side to it which you can now round off with the back of the pointed tool. Take your time – and for goodness' sake, keep breathing! Once rounded, both front and back, add 'waists' between the knuckles to add character and shadows to the fingers.

8 Turn the palm of the hand upwards, and using the ball end of the wooden tool, rock it into the flat part to create a depression.

9 With the blade of the wooden tool, mark a line at the wrist.

10 Check that the wrist is small enough. If not, roll it through your fingers to slim it down.

11 Flatten the wrist slightly to make it look realistic.

12 Take the side of the blade of the wooden tool and scrape a tiny amount of clay downwards on each side of the wrist, then back upwards again to create the bones of the wrist. It may sound fussy, I know, but it's the detail that gives the hand life.

13 Look at your thumbs to see how they actually work with the hand. It's a digit we tend to deride, and say someone is 'all thumbs', but it's an incredibly flexible and useful part of the hand – so let's give it the same credit we do the rest.

14 To begin, make an elongated tadpole clay shape, and squash the head end to make the thumb pad. Run the metal ball tool over the pad to thin the edges all round, and fit the thumb onto the hand.

15 Smooth out with the wooden tool and mark in the thumbnail.

16 Take the ball tool to work the back of the hands. Work the thin wire part of the tool to separate the base of the fingers again, and drag the ball end between the base and the knuckle area.

17 Make a fist with your own hand to see where the knuckles fall (much lower than you thought, eh?) Round off the knuckle base and run some shallow lines down the hand to give an impression of veins. Turn the hand over and mark the fingers, the creases at the base of the fingers and lines in your hands.

18 Pose the hand against the figure you intend it for, and sever the forearm to length. Round off the cut edge.

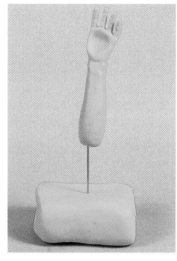

Step 12

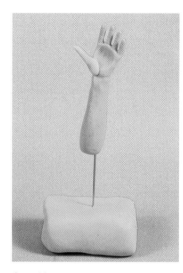

Step 14

Step 16

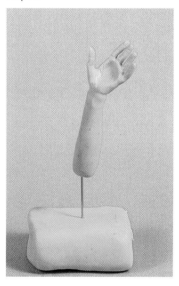

Step 17

The finished hand

19 Finally you will need to make a hole for the wire.

20 Take a deep breath, and start immediately on the other hand while the process is fresh in your mind.

Remember, whichever hand you made first, you now need to make the other one. That's obvious, but keep a large pillow to hand to scream into when you find you've just done two perfect lefts.

LOWER LEGS AND FEET

Most period figures have their lower legs covered, and it's tempting to simplify these to a rough, basic shape. However, if you master them properly it's easy to make a mould and adapt the foot as and when you

and females. Notice, too, how the lower leg is set back from the upper; it doesn't run downwards in a straight line.

1 Model the legs and feet separately, in rough first, to get the size correct.

2 Scratch the joins at the ankle to key the pieces, then smooth the leg onto the foot. Keep comparing them to make sure that you have got a left and right. It won't be that apparent on the figure if you get it wrong, but it will irritate the eye.

3 Work on a flat foot first of all. The clay will work just like a real foot and bend to fit a shoe shape.

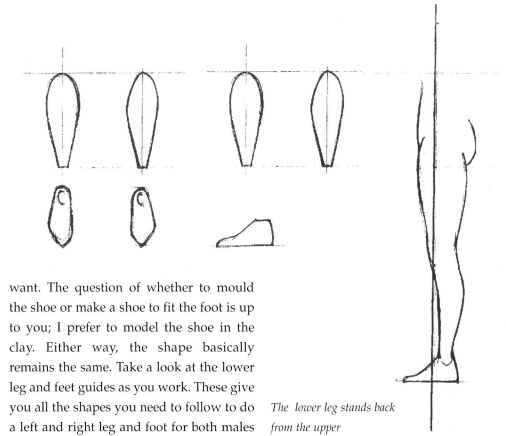

Guides for the lower legs and feet

The lower leg stands back from the upper

want. The question of whether to mould the shoe or make a shoe to fit the foot is up to you; I prefer to model the shoe in the clay. Either way, the shape basically remains the same. Take a look at the lower leg and feet guides as you work. These give you all the shapes you need to follow to do a left and right leg and foot for both males

CHECK LIST

Check that:

• the calf muscle is higher at the out-side of the leg.

• the Achilles tendon is clearly defined with depressions on either side.

• the ankle bones are defined, with the inside bone protruding forwards more than the outside.

• the shin bone connects to the bones leading to the big toe.

• the arch of the foot is on the inside.

• the feet are not too small. Feet come in all sizes but these feet need to carry the weight of the figure, so don't make them too little.

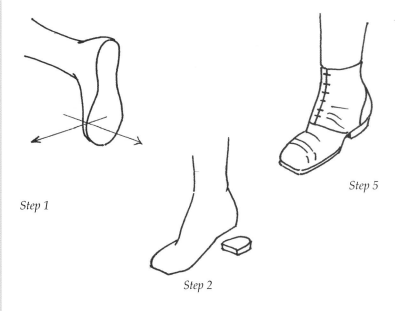

Step 1

Step 2

Step 5

And you thought feet were simple! You now have a choice: you can either make a mould now, or using your tools, work the shoe shape.

SHAPING THE SHOE

1 Take a metal tool, flatten the sole of the foot slightly, and then run the tool around the edge of the foot. You will need to go back and forth to get this edge sharp and clear. Shape the toe of the shoe to suit the style of footwear.

2 Add a suitable heel to the shoe, again depending on the style.

3 You can now add the detail. Mark a fine line around the edge of the foot to define the sole and upper.

4 Mark in the line between the shoe and the foot. Work a tiny depression up the foot, away from the shoe edge, to represent the thickness of the leather.

5 Create creases in the shoe over the toes and around the ankle according to the wear of the leather and, if you would like to add further detail, sketch in laces or buttons.

Shaping the shoe

Arms and legs ready for wiring to the figure

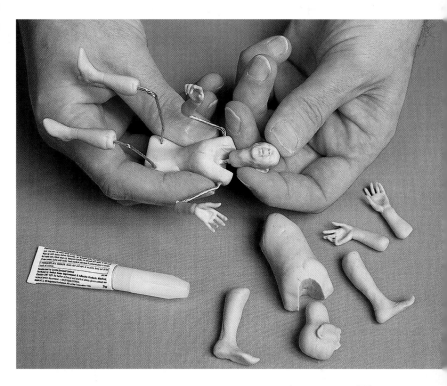

Facial Details and EXPRESSIONS

The Young Wife

FACIAL DETAILS

EYES

The eyes are the most fascinating feature of the face; the one poets write about and the one lovers moon about. They are also the part of the face that we have perhaps the most difficulty sculpting.

To keep it simple, the eyeball is a sphere set into a bony cavity in which it is only partly visible through two folds of skin called the eyelids.

The eye is closed or opened by the action of the upper lid, like a roller blind. The lower lid is mainly inactive, and only moves when the cheek muscle pushes it. When the eye is open, the curve of the upper lid is longer and more rounded than the lower lid.

The eye and its lids are rounded, not a flat plane set on the face; they are deeper above and below, and at either side. Take a look at the illustrations (see page 92) to see how this action alters the face.

Generally, women's eyes are larger than men's, and set in a softer, more rounded socket. Men's eyes, in contrast, often have a more pronounced brow above.

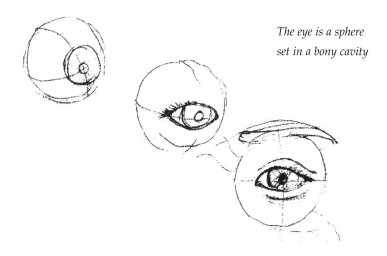

The eye is a sphere set in a bony cavity

Take into account that make-up, the way the eyebrow is painted, and the direction of the iris, can change the look of the eye.

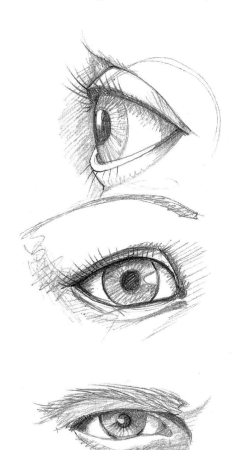

Generally, women have rounder, softer eyes than men

EXERCISE

Only dolls have perfectly symmetrical eyes; human eyes are quite lopsided. To see for yourself, take a mirror and place it on its edge down the middle of a photograph of a face you know well so that one side of the face is reflected. The image will be perfectly symmetrical, but look nothing like the real person. This is not an excuse to do Picasso-style faces!

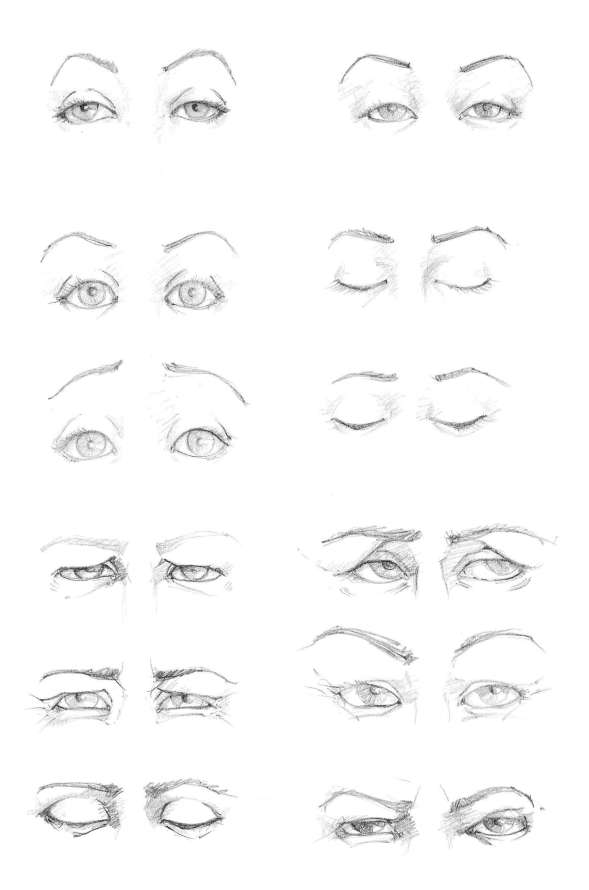

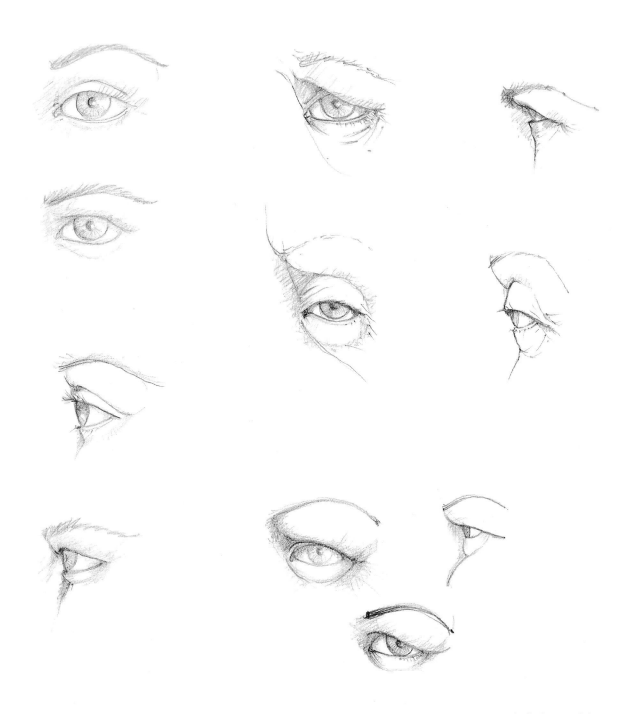

*The flesh around the
eyes makes each
setting different*

*The upper eyelid opens and closes
like a roller blind, while the lower
lid remains inactive*

*A selection of
nose shapes*

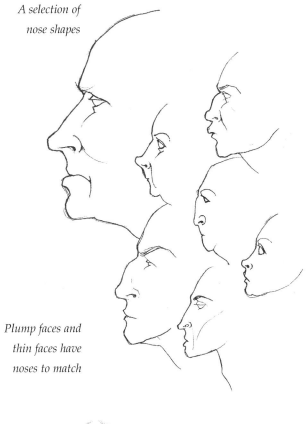

*Plump faces and
thin faces have
noses to match*

NOSE

Unlike the eyes, the nose has a life of its own; it makes its own rules and grows with the face. Sometimes cute, sometimes sexy, but more often than not, it is simply the butt of countless jokes. The nose has a hard time of it.

The nose starts between the eyes and continues to the lips; it is not a separate unit stuck on. The nostrils have life; they can be made to narrow or flare out by pressure from the upper lip and cheeks.

Plump faces and thin faces may also have noses to match. There are lots of shapes and sizes.

*Nostrils come in different shapes, and have a life of
their own*

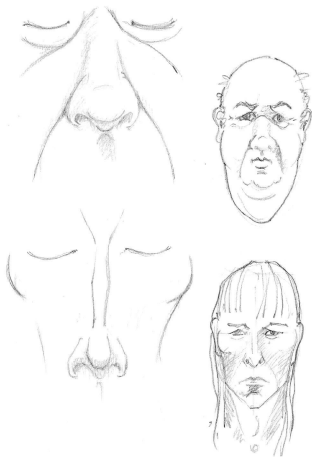

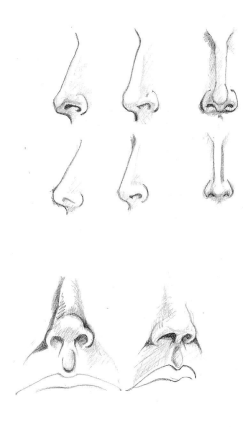

*The nose is not a separate unit tagged onto the
face. It starts at the eyes and continues to the lips*

LIPS

Like the eyes, the lips are situated on a curved surface of the face and supported by the teeth (or not, as the case may be).

The upper lip is composed of three parts – two tapering segments at the side, filled in at the middle by a shield shape which connects the upper mouth part and the nostrils. The top edge of the upper lip is sharply defined.

The lower lip is made up of two tapering pads set in a larger pad, which continues down the sides of the mouth and chin. There is no defined line on this lip, just colour. The upper lip sits over the lower lip.

Men tend to have thinner lips than women, although this is by no means the rule. If you want to sculpt full lips on a male figure to effect a sensual look, make sure that the other features are equally strongly defined, otherwise you may create a look of petulance or sulkiness instead.

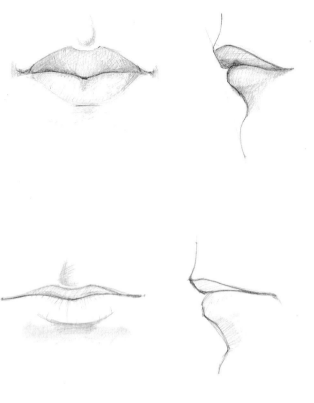

Generally, women have fuller lips than men. For both, however, the upper lip protrudes over the lower

EXERCISE

Practise these features on a piece of clay. Don't try to make a face; you simply want to learn how the shapes are formed in isolation.

The upper lip is composed of three sections, and the lower lip of two

95

FACIAL EXPRESSIONS

There are six basic categories of facial expression: sadness, anger, joy, fear, disgust and surprise. They are pretty much universal, regardless of an individual's cultural background. If the face alone is shown, we can make an educated guess as to what the facial expression means and probably be right, but get an even better idea if the body is also visible.

One of the best sources for these facial expressions are magazines; some are better for male expressions, and others for female ones. Sports pages and magazines on sport subjects are good for male faces, whereas you can try television guides, especially the film section, but beware, these faces belong to actors who offer a self-conscious version of expressions. For younger female faces, fan magazines often offer good examples of an extremely passionate face which can be a good source for study.

Look carefully at certain stories and notice how a simple facial expression can sometimes be misused to tell a biased story. This is often the case with photographs of politicians and the Royal Family. Simply rubbing the eye to remove a piece of dust can be described as weeping in a story that wants us to believe what the newspaper want us to believe.

The face alone might convey different meanings to different people. Greed can be misinterpreted as lust. Expectation can look like the person is shocked (the 'goosed' expression). We've all met shy people, and some might think of it as deviousness. Think, and look for photos of vanity, or of stupidity, suspicion, disappointment, and flirtation. See how the body helps to tell the story behind each. Add these expressions to your collection.

EXERCISE

Take a photograph in a magazine, and cut out the whole of the person – the editor will have selected a picture which basically conveys as much as possible of what he or she wants us to know about the news story behind the photograph.

Write down on the photo what you have been told is happening in the image, and then take a subjective view of what else the individual could be doing. Look carefully, and ask yourself if the body is telling the same story as the face. Rubbing the eye is a simple action involving the fingers and eye, whereas weeping tenses the shoulders and affects the whole body.

Miss Havisham

There are sometimes expressions of mood that perhaps only our best friends are able to spot. They know us well, and are able to notice a change in the face we normally show to 'the world'. As adults, we are able to hide most of our moods. Emotions, on the other hand, take us by surprise and our faces and bodies react to the overwhelming stimulation of the moment. Someone who experiences the emotion of fear is affected in a very physical way, but the mood of anxiety can be hidden quite well, and only spotted in an indirect way. Look around at the people you know well, and try to see if you can identify the mood they are in. (Falling in love is one emotion we think we can all see in someone, but take care – they might have had a total lobotomy.)

Remember, your figures are most likely to end up in a room setting, even if this is a simple 'prop', and with care, this will help to enhance the mood of the finished piece and give a further clue to the emotions of the figure or group of figures.

SCULPTING THE FACIAL EXPRESSIONS

As you work the different kinds of moods or emotions, think about your own unique observations of people's faces and features, and use the text and the images provided here to guide you.

EXERCISE

Think of a character from a book, and a scene in which that character expresses the emotion or mood which is most telling. Fix the scene in your mind before you start, otherwise you may find yourself getting confused and changing the scene to suit the expression. Try a character like Dickens' Miss Havisham from *Great Expectations*. Think about if you have been influenced more by the book or by one of the many film versions (be careful though, this could give your age away faster than anything). In your version is she haughty and proud, angry or victimized, a survivor of circumstance, or bitter with life experience. Perhaps she is just plain batty. I didn't know myself just how affected I was by Martita Hunt's portrayal until I heard the latest director say that he had decided not to use cobwebs in her scenes. What nonsense, I thought, then realized that I think of her as a bejewelled spider: vindictive, cruel, lonely and sad.

MATERIALS AND EQUIPMENT

CLAY

CLEAN TILE OR BAKING SHEET

TOOLS

ACETONE

CRYING

THE OPEN-MOUTH CRY

THE MOUTH

The muscles pull the mouth open wide, wrapping the lips tightly around the side of the teeth and jaw. This causes deep ropes (rolls of fat or muscle) to form at both sides, and the chin to rise, flatten and roughen. The lips are thin, covering the upper teeth. The lower lip rises at the centre, falling away at the sides, and allowing the teeth here to show.

THE NOSE

Because the muscles of the cheek stretch outwards and upwards, the tip of the nose and the nostrils stretch out to the side.

THE EYES AND BROWS

The brows lower and form together at the centre, causing furrows between and across. The eyes tightly compress, and deep crow's-feet appear at the sides of each. A slight bag forms under the eyes.

1 Since the lips are stretched tightly to the side, the first action is to remove the lips from the basic face. Smooth the lips outwards from the centre, remembering that the teeth are like a small tube, and that the lips are being pulled back as well as to the sides.

2 Drag the spare clay into the apple of the cheeks.

3 Cut a slit across the division of the lips. Push a small wooden tool into it, and roughly shape the mouth into a square, gaping hole (you're not mining for gold, so don't cut too deep).

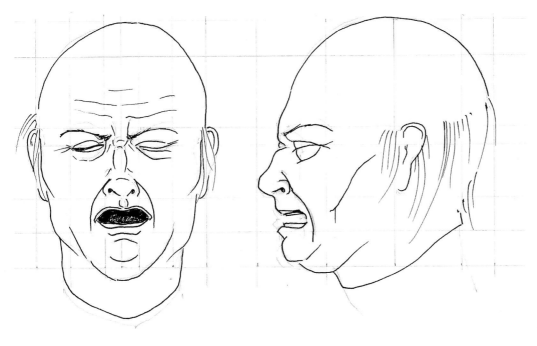

The open-mouth and closed-mouth cry

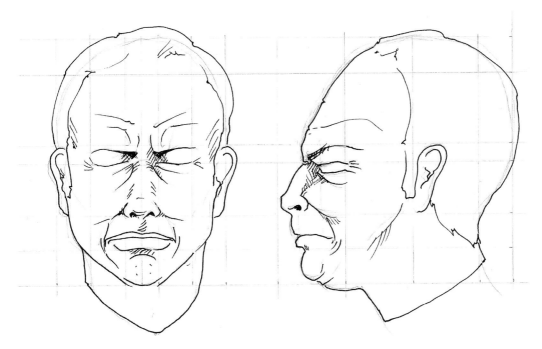

4 Slightly squash the chin, and sketch in where you think the creases may form.

5 With your tool, spread the nostrils slightly, and deepen the creases that appear at either side of the nose.

6 Smooth the eyelids downwards and upwards. Remember that here the lower lid is being moved by the cheek muscles. Make a slit where the eyelids meet, and continue outwards with the tool to mark in crow's-feet.

7 Drag the brows downwards a bit, particularly at the centre, to form a roll, and mark in deep creases across the top of the nose, and upwards between the brows.

8 Having sketched in the movement of the muscles, go over your work, refining and smoothing until you are satisfied with it, and checking the profile as you do so.

9 To finish the facial expression, make a tiny pair of dentures for the side teeth, and place into the required position.

10 Remove any finger marks with a wash of acetone, and redefine the creases if they have lost their clarity, then bake the figure in the oven.

THE CLOSED-MOUTH CRY

THE MOUTH

Most of the action takes place on the lower lip. The mouth flattens around the curve of the teeth causing deep dimples to occur at either side of the mouth. The chin makes this clear; it forms into a ball, producing a deep crease under the lower lip.

THE NOSE

The nose remains normal.

THE EYES AND BROWS

The eyes and brows compress as before.

1 Smooth the mouth out as before, but this time the cheeks are not so rounded, so it's more a case of rounding out the lips.

2 Squash the chin as before, but now form a ridge to make a small, round ball with a deep crease above it curving under the bottom lip.

3 Make dimples around the outside edges of the lips.

4 Leave the nose as it is because it does not change in the closed-mouth cry.

5 Follow the same format for the eyes and brows as before.

6 Refine and finish as before and then bake the figure in the normal way.

ANGER AND RAGE

THE MOUTH

The upper lip is stretched and raised to show the upper teeth. The distance between the nose and lip is shortened. The centre of the upper lip is wide and curled before it turns down to meet the lower lip, which can mirror the upper lip, or be more round or square. Whatever you choose, the lower teeth show between. The chin is sharply defined, with a deep crease between the lower lip and the ball shape of the chin.

THE NOSE

As with the open-mouth cry, the nostrils flare but much more so, causing a sneer and resulting in deep creases at either side of the nose.

THE EYES AND BROWS

The eyes widen, particularly at the top outer edge. The brows lower and combine into creases, similar to the crying eye.

1 As with the open-mouth cry, the lips pull across and around the teeth, so smooth the lips outwards and upwards, dragging the clay into the cheeks.

2 Cut a slit for the opening of the mouth with a metal tool.

3 With a wooden tool, open up the lips, pushing the clay into the shape you require. Remember that the upper lip is shorter than normal at the centre.

4 Define the ball of the chin. It is very sharply defined in these emotions.

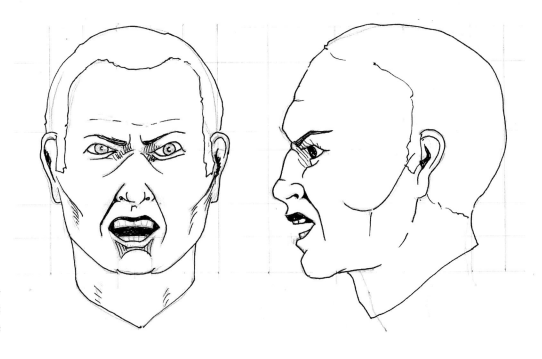

*Expressions of rage,
and anger with
compressed lips*

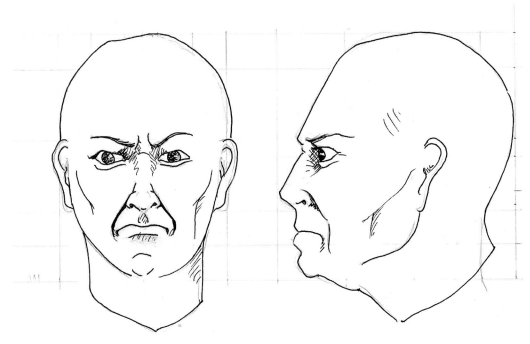

5 Open up the nostrils to flare outwards. This action on the face pushes up the flesh above, causing the sneer to start here and run into the deep crease around the mouth. It is a simple, but vital feature to give the expression its meaning.

6 Lift the outer top edge of the eyes slightly, and exaggerate the crease on the upper eyelid to follow this new line, keeping it low at the centre. Drag the clay between the eyes downwards, and form the crease over the nose and upwards.

7 Make a pair of dentures into the shape of two small orange segments, and place in position.

8 Lightly mark in the teeth as before, and place into position, checking the profile as you work.

9 Refine, wash with acetone, then bake in the normal way.

ANGER, COMPRESSED LIPS

THE MOUTH

The lips compress and almost disappear into a thin, rounded line curving down at the sides into short, sharp creases. The pad of the lower lip is clearly defined, and the chin flattens into a dimpled surface, or forms a clear ball shape.

THE NOSE

The nose remains as normal, but the creases on either side drag downwards.

THE EYES AND BROWS

The face tries to control the rage. In doing this, the eyes widen and the brows lower, but level into a fixed line. The more out of the control the emotion becomes, the more the eyes widen and brows lower.

1 Flatten the lips outwards, but this time downwards, too.

2 Take off more clay from the upper lip, leaving a pad on the lower. The upper lip holds tightly to the teeth.

3 Now define the chin and the lower lip. With your tool, form a wide, curved hollow over the chin to create the padded roll shape of the lower lip, which flows outwards to the jaw line.

4 Mark in the crease at the outer edge of the lips.

5 The nose remains as normal, but with your tool, form creases at either side. According to the type of face you are working on, you can make hollows appear under the cheekbones.

6 Work the eyes and brows as you have for rage. If the face is trying to control the anger, leave out the brow creases. .

7 Check the profile as you work, making sure you are happy with it.

8 Refine, wash with acetone, then bake in the normal way.

HAPPINESS

LAUGHTER

Considering they are opposing emotions, rage and laughter are surprisingly similar in appearance on the face.

THE MOUTH

The mouth opens and stretches in the same way as for rage, pulling the lips close around the teeth, except that the corners of the mouth lift and the muscle tension does not occur, pulling the lips into a square. This time, the mouth is composed of gently rhythmical curves. The upper teeth are clearly visible, and show the individual's style of teeth, small or large, and in certain cases, the teeth and gum line show.

The chin pulls down. The hinge effect that pulls the chin into the neck causes a chin strap (a roll of fat) to form.

THE NOSE

The nostrils flare, but in a relaxed manner, and the nose tends to squash. The entire cheek lifts padding up the side of the face, causing an S shape to form in profile, from the eye to chin. Creases form under the cheeks and continue around the chin into the strap.

THE EYES AND BROWS

The eyes usually close and the action of the cheeks pushes up the lower lid to form a roll under the eye, which in turn makes the lower lid curve upwards. This is what gives the eye its laughter, as opposed to tears.

The brows are relaxed, but not curved. With the overjoyed look, the brows raise and the forehead creases.

1 Form the open mouth exactly as for the open-mouth cry or for rage, but this time drag the clay upwards to form high,

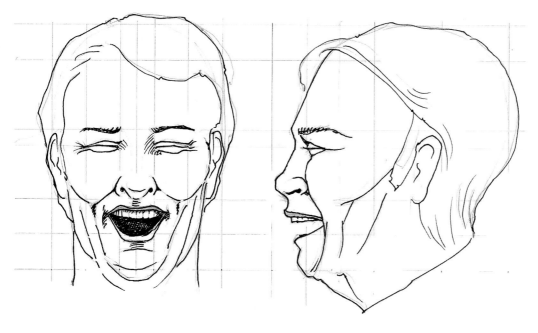

*Expressions of
laughter and smiling*

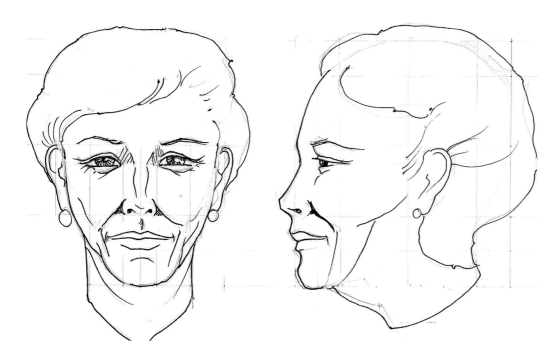

wide cheeks. Make sure that the chin swings downwards and into the neck. You may have to add a banana-shaped piece of clay to form the chin strap. Blend this in well, but retain the roll effect. For plump to fat faces, this can start from the side of the cheeks to under the ear and continue all the way down to the base of the neck. If the

head is thrown back, the chin strap does not occur.

2 Slightly flatten and broaden the base of the nose, and cut in the deep creases around the mouth. Unlike rage, these lines are broad and curving, and continue down to the chin.

3 Check the profile to see that you are getting the S-shaped curve.

4 Smooth out the original eye line. Make the tiniest pad of clay you have ever made, and cover the eye with it. Yes I know, getting two to match is almost impossible, so don't blend them in until you are satisfied that they are reasonably equal.

4 With a metal tool, cut a line where the eyelids meet, making sure that it has an upward curve.

5 Cut a line under each eye to form a roll, and mark in the wrinkles at the outer edge of them.

6 The brows remain relaxed and normal. With the overjoyed look, the brow edge is raised and the lines form on the forehead. The eyes may be half open.

7 Refine, and wash with acetone before baking in the oven.

SMILING

THE MOUTH

A gentle, closed-mouth smile simply needs the outside corners to turn up a little, and to curve around the teeth slightly. The broader the smile, the wider the mouth and the rounder the cheeks, causing more creases and dimples to appear. Therefore, the rounder the cheeks, the bigger the roll that appears under the eye. The teeth may, or may not, show.

WORKING THE SMILE INTO OTHER EXPRESSIONS

The only emotion to have a relaxed brow is the smile, so it figures that if you add some tension to the brow, you will get some very complex expressions. Try playing with these when you come to paint on the brows, you will be amazed at how you can change the expression with a single line of colour.

Lowered brow = slyness

Raised brow with forehead creases = eagerness

Straight brow with middle creases = false humility

Brow droops at the outer edge = happiness, or sadness

1 A hint of a smile is made by simply pushing the tip of the wooden tool into the corners of the mouth, causing tiny folds to form at the outer edge of the lips.

2 Slight rolls may start to appear under the eye. Take the wooden tool and create a curved line under the bag of the eye, and push it up slightly.

3 As the smile broadens, the expression approaches laughter. Use a mirror to see how your own face changes from a smile to a laugh. If you have two mirrors this is even better, because then you can check the profile.

SURPRISE

THE RELAXED MOUTH

The jaw drops with its own weight, with all the muscles relaxed in the open-mouthed expression of surprise. There are no stress lines around the cheeks and jaw.

THE PURSED MOUTH

The pursed mouth is a tight-lipped look. The lip corners draw together, making two exaggerated pillows, clearly defining the formation of the lips, three parts to the upper lip and two to the lower. The cheeks suck in and show the line of the cheekbone. Lines fan outwards from the mouth.

   The relaxed surprised mouth could be a beauty contest winner, and the pursed-mouth look could be when she has just been goosed by the judge!

THE NOSE

The nose remains relaxed.

THE EYES AND BROWS

Wide open and round eyes are the clue to the surprised look. Add on raised eyebrows and you have got the idea. The iris is clearly visible, and there is a lot of the white of the eye showing.

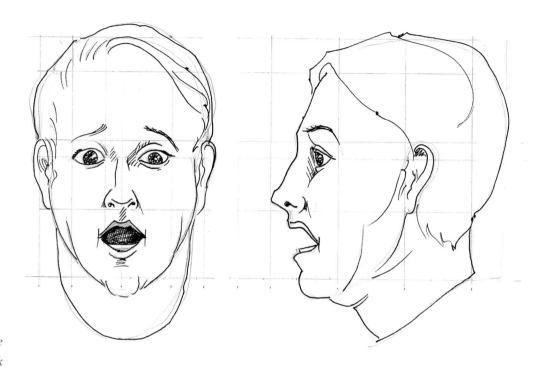

Surprise, and the pursed-mouth look

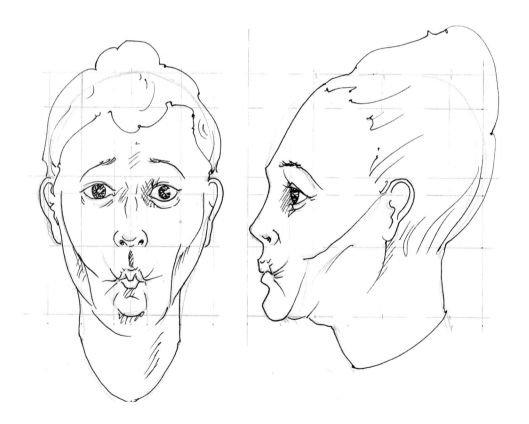

SURPRISE

1 Cut a slit in the mouth between the lips to the width of the relaxed mouth. Unlike rage and laughter, the mouth does not stretch wide.

2 With a wooden tool, open up the mouth, pulling the mouth apart and downwards.

3 The upper lip remains relaxed so does not need altering.

4 Pull the chin down towards the neck. The fatter the face, the more a chin strap forms. To make a chin strap, roll a crescent shape in clay and smooth on under the chin, to just behind the ears.

5 Using your tool, neatly define the ball of the chin.

6 Leave the nose as it is because it does not change.

7 With a wooden tool, push the upper eyelid upwards to round the eye a little; too much and it will look as if the eyes are literally popping out of the head. Remember that the iris will be painted as a round ball which will add the finishing touch to the look of surprise.

8 Generally, no creases form on the brow. Try the expression in a mirror, and 'feel' what happens. To me, it feels as if my scalp has been tightened with the ears pulled backwards. Don't think of this when you're in the street; you may find you are doing it and it could look rather odd to say the least.

THE PURSED MOUTH

1 This is best done with a mirror, in private. Imagine that you have just sat on something very cold and wet. Feel how the insides of your cheeks are pulled into the space between the teeth, which are slightly parted. See how this action flattens the outside of the cheeks against the side of the face. The deepest point is at the corners of the mouth, causing a round pad above and below the lips. Copy this onto the figure.

2 Make lines fanning outwards from the corners of the mouth.

3 Make the lips draw in and form three balls at the top and two balls at the bottom. To give a real 'Ooh!' look, make a small, round hole in the middle of the lips.

DISGUST

THE MOUTH

The upper lip raises and flattens to give a sneer, causing deep furrows to appear on either side of the nose. The lower lip also raises and pulls against the lower teeth. The chin flattens and wrinkles. The jaw squashes

against the neck as the head tries to pull away from the object of disgust, forming a chin strap to appear.

THE NOSE

The deep creases made by the lips lift the sides of the nose, flattening the nose tip which tends to point downwards. The appearance is squashed and broadened.

THE EYES AND BROWS

The eyes are compressed tightly shut, and the raised cheeks form long, flat creases underneath. The brows draw downwards and together, forming creases between the brows and over the nose. Horizontal creases form at the outer edges of the eye, too.

1 Smooth out the chin upwards and sideways to form a raised, upside-down U-shaped sausage shape under the lower lip.

2 Make a crescent-shaped roll of clay for the chin strap, and smooth it firmly into position.

3 Wrinkle the chin slightly, making sure it looks natural.

4 Flatten and raise the upper lip into a square, taking the excess clay into the creases at either side of the mouth.

5 Continue the crease line formed around the upper mouth over the nostrils, and cut a deep line to define. Remember that the lips are drawn tightly across the upper teeth. Flare the nostrils and flatten the nose.

6 Pull a little of the clay upwards under the eye to straighten the line and form a horizontal bag.

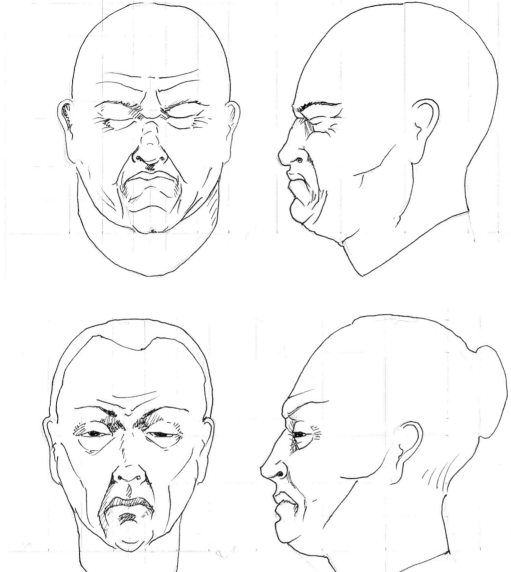

*Expressions of
disgust and disdain*

7 Drag the clay downwards above the eye to close the lids, pulling the inside edge of the brows together to make creases between the eyes and over the nose.

8 Draw in deepish frown lines all the way across the forehead.

DISDAIN
The lower half of the face is the same as the disgusted face, but the upper part is less compressed. The eyes are half open to view the object of disdain, and the brows raised.

1 Begin by working the mouth area and the nose as you have for the expression of disgust.

2 Drag down the upper lid to close the eye, and form a rounded bag under the eye.

3 The brow area tends to be raised, but drawn together, so taking your tool, form a crease above and between the brows to combine with the creases on the forehead.

FEAR

THE MOUTH

The opposite of the smile, the lower lip stretches tight and straight into the jaw, to form deep creases at the side of the mouth. The upper lip is relaxed, covering the upper teeth. The lower teeth are visible at the outer edge where the lips are drawn down. The centre of the lower lip may be raised slightly to cover the teeth.

The action of the mouth causes the chin to flatten and raise up to form an oval ball shape.

Although the upper lip is relaxed, the tension of the lower lip pulls the lip close to the teeth and causes lines to form from the nose round the mouth.

The cheeks are pulled inwards to form a couple of hollows.

THE NOSE

The nose is relaxed, but well-defined due to the stress on the mouth.

THE EYES AND BROWS

The eyes are round and wide open. The brows appear almost level, but pull together to form folds in-between. The forehead has straight lines across it. The less fear being experienced and exhibited, the less the exaggeration in the facial features.

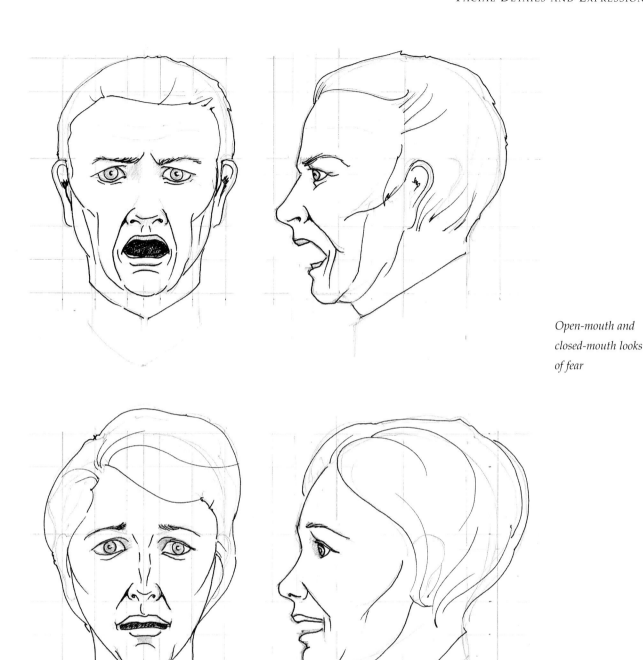

Open-mouth and closed-mouth looks of fear

1 Smooth out the lips in a downward motion to start the expression. Make a cut a little wider than for the relaxed mouth.

2 With a wooden tool, pull the lower lip into shape. Smooth the upper lip across and down to join the outer edges of the lower lip.

3 With your tool, flatten the chin over the jaw and form a deep crease under the lower lip and over the oval ball shape of the chin.

4 Finally, push in two bracket-shaped creases on either side of the lower part of the mouth.

113

5 Mark in the creases from the nostrils to the mouth.

6 Hollow the cheeks, unless the face is very plump.

7 If necessary, make tiny dentures for the lower teeth. You may find you have enough spare clay inside the mouth to suggest these.

8 The nose is relaxed but, due to the strain either side, the nose may appear slightly sharper and more clearly defined.

9 Take a wooden tool and push up the upper eyelid to round the eyes slightly. The action involved in the mouth pulling downwards has a tendency to stretch the skin underneath the eyes, and pulls down the lower lid a fraction. It may also give definition to the area underneath the eye socket as the bag is stretched a bit. If you make a curved crease with your tool, it will define this.

10 Form creases between the eyebrows to represent furrows on the forehead.

DROWSINESS

THE MOUTH

The mouth is relaxed, but may tend to droop slightly.

THE NOSE

The nose remains relaxed.

THE EYES AND BROWS

The eyes are half closed. In trying to fight sleep, the eyebrows raise, causing furrows to appear on the forehead and bags to form under the eyes. This will be made much more obvious when the eyes are painted to show the iris half covered, and the pupil partially blocked.

The drowsy look of the eyes, coupled with a smile, can be used for a lecherous or drunken expression.

1 The mouth is relaxed. With the point of the wooden tool, make a tiny prod at the corners to give a slight smile when placed at the upper mouth, and a slight droop if placed at the lower edge.

2 The nose remains relaxed so does not require alteration.

3 Drag a little clay downwards over the upper eyelid, and mark a gently curved line.

4 Mark in the eye bags that appear under the eyes.

5 Smooth over the brow line to lift it and mark in the furrows on the forehead.

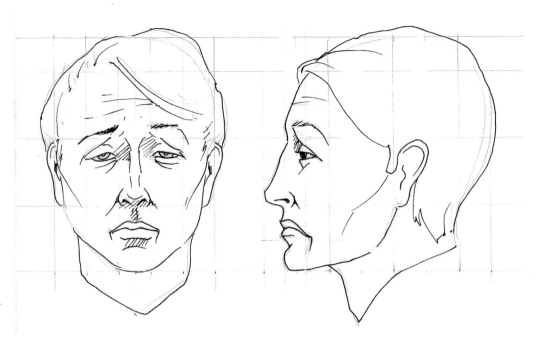

Expressions of drowsiness

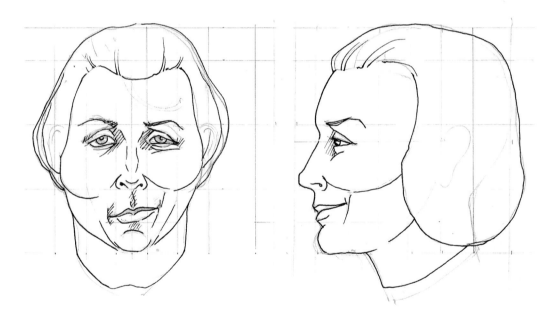

SLEEP

To do the expression of sleep, the mouth and nose should be formed as they are for the look of drowsiness. The mouth may drop open in a relaxed manner. (With the right position of the body, this can also resemble a sensuous, passionate look.) The eyelids are closed and the eyebrows remain relaxed.

1 The mouth and nose are the same as for drowsiness if the mouth is to be closed. If the mouth is to be open, make a slit and prise open with a wooden tool. The open mouth is very relaxed in sleep and causes no creases or lines to form.

2 Drag the clay over the eye to smooth out, and cut a sharp, curving line to

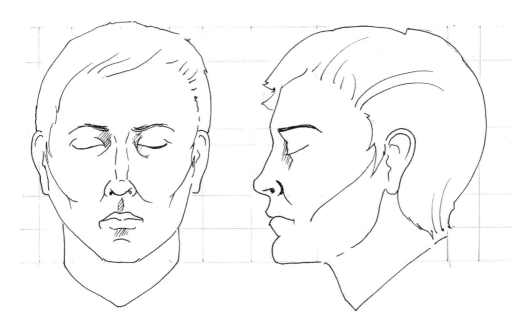

Sleep

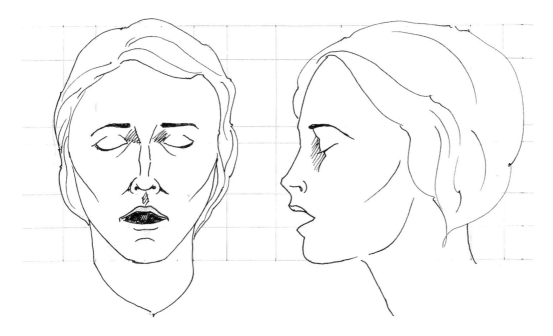

define the meeting of the two lids. Take a fraction of the clay away from underneath the eye to make the upper eyelid appear to overlap the lower one.

3 Mark in the eye bags that appear under the eyes.

4 The brows are relaxed so do not require alteration.

5 When in sleep, the head often rolls forward, causing a pronounced chin strap to form. To do this, add a crescent of clay to the chin, and blend.

Finishing
THE FIGURE

A Windy Day

No Better Than They Should Be

A T LAST YOU CAN BEGIN TO SEE *what you have created. It is also the point at which you see what you could have done, but that's the way to learn really. Each time I make a figure I get an idea for another one – how I can twist the head a little or lift a shoulder a fraction to give more movement to the figure. I've been known to take notes for future projects (not often) and you may like to do this, too.*

WIRING AND PADDING

Wiring and padding couldn't be simpler, but do remember to be generous with the wire when you first cut it; you can always trim it down. It's the law that if you fix them and find that you've made them too short, it will be the time when the glue sticks better than ever before.

Try to get picture wire if you can. The multi-strand character of the wire will take a lot of bending, whereas the single-strand wire can be fragile at the point of the bend.

MAKING YOUR OWN WIRE
Metal merchants will stock fine brass wire. Do not be tempted to use copper wire, it's far too soft.

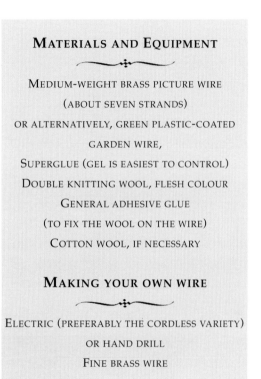

MATERIALS AND EQUIPMENT

MEDIUM-WEIGHT BRASS PICTURE WIRE
(ABOUT SEVEN STRANDS)
OR ALTERNATIVELY, GREEN PLASTIC-COATED
GARDEN WIRE,
SUPERGLUE (GEL IS EASIEST TO CONTROL)
DOUBLE KNITTING WOOL, FLESH COLOUR
GENERAL ADHESIVE GLUE
(TO FIX THE WOOL ON THE WIRE)
COTTON WOOL, IF NECESSARY

MAKING YOUR OWN WIRE

ELECTRIC (PREFERABLY THE CORDLESS VARIETY)
OR HAND DRILL
FINE BRASS WIRE

1 Depending on the thickness of the wire, cut six or seven strands; about 6ft (2m) will be fine. Try to trap the ends under a weight as you cut them, or you could end up being entangled in wire spaghetti.

2 Twist one end together very firmly and place over a hook, getting someone to hold the other end.

3 Smooth your hand along the wire to even it out and twist this end together, again very firmly.

4 Slip the twist of wires over another hook fixed into a drill. You can use either an electric or hand drill , but I find that an electric cordless drill, set at a low speed, is the easiest to control for doing this job.

5 Start the drill, pulling tightly against the wire to make it taut. As it twists, the wire will shorten so be prepared to move in with it.

6 Stop the drill and relax the tension to see how firm it is; you don't need to overdo it.

> ### TIP
>
> If you are also a furniture maker, this makes a great metal trim for edges, especially if you use a mixture of wires.

MAKING UP THE FIGURE

1 Lay the units on the proportion chart, making any adjustments in height that are necessary.

2 Carefully measure the spaces in between, allowing for the wire that goes into the body. Cut the wire to this length, adding a little extra just to be safe.

3 Glue the wires into the body first. Try on the feet and adjust the length to fit, making sure that the legs are the same length and that the feet are on the correct leg. Glue them into position.

Step 3. Gluing the wires into the body

4 Then repeat the whole process again with the arms.

5 Begin the padding. Smear a little glue over one arm wire and place on the wool, winding it round and round and up and down. Glue the end to fix. Be warned: it's hugely tempting to pack it in at the ends. Don't; it will pull the wires out better than any other way I know.

6 Do the other arm. Bend the arms upwards, well out of the way while you do the legs. (Hooking the wool over your figure's precious fingers is mind-blowingly frustrating.)

7 Glue and wind wool around each leg as for the arms. You may wish to add some cotton wool padding after the first wind to save wool and time. Once complete, squeeze the thighs into shape and set the knee slightly back to give a realistic curve to the leg.

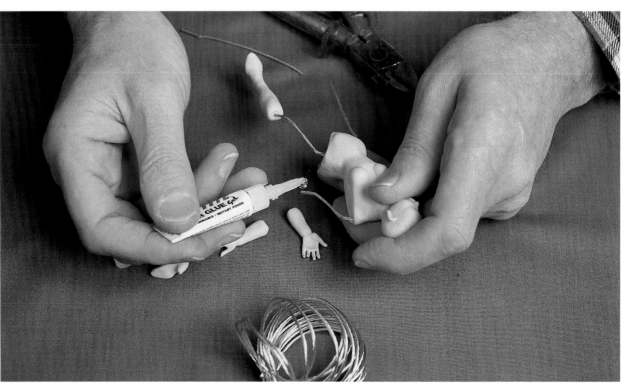

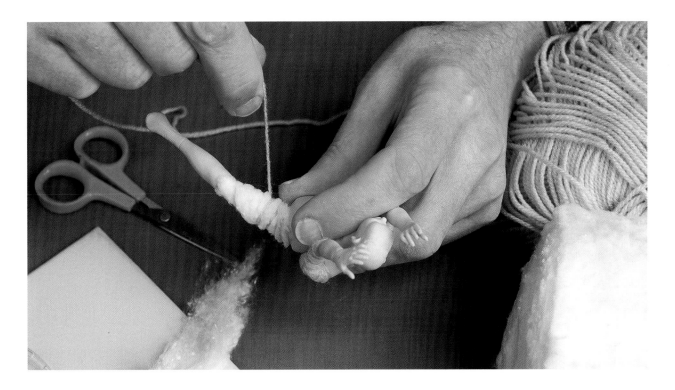

EXERCISE

Observe what happens to the human figure in extreme positions. It's easy and fun to do. Learn to sketch very roughly like I've done (see page 124) (don't worry about proportions at this stage, it's just an exercise in freedom). Drawing the body in simple units, without the padding of flesh and muscles, will give you an idea of what happens underneath. Look through magazines and books for ideas. Place some tracing paper over a photograph and see if you can draw a very simple skeleton beneath the clothing. Keep your drawings and photographs in a scrapbook as you do them. Don't wait until you can draw like Leonardo da Vinci – your first attempts, viewed later, will have a charm of their own and should be treasured.

ADDING MORE MOVEMENT TO YOUR FIGURE

If you want to make a figure that can take a variety of poses, you will need to make spaces in your original figure to take in more wires.

1 Model the figure as normal, with the head, neck and torso as one piece.

2 Cut out the area between the shoulders and down into the torso.

3 Shorten the clay neck stump and round it off.

4 Cut out a section across the body at the waist and round off the two ends.

5 Push a pin into the neck, leaving a short end protruding, and place it onto the torso to mark the wire holes into the torso. Remove the pin and make proper holes to take the wires.

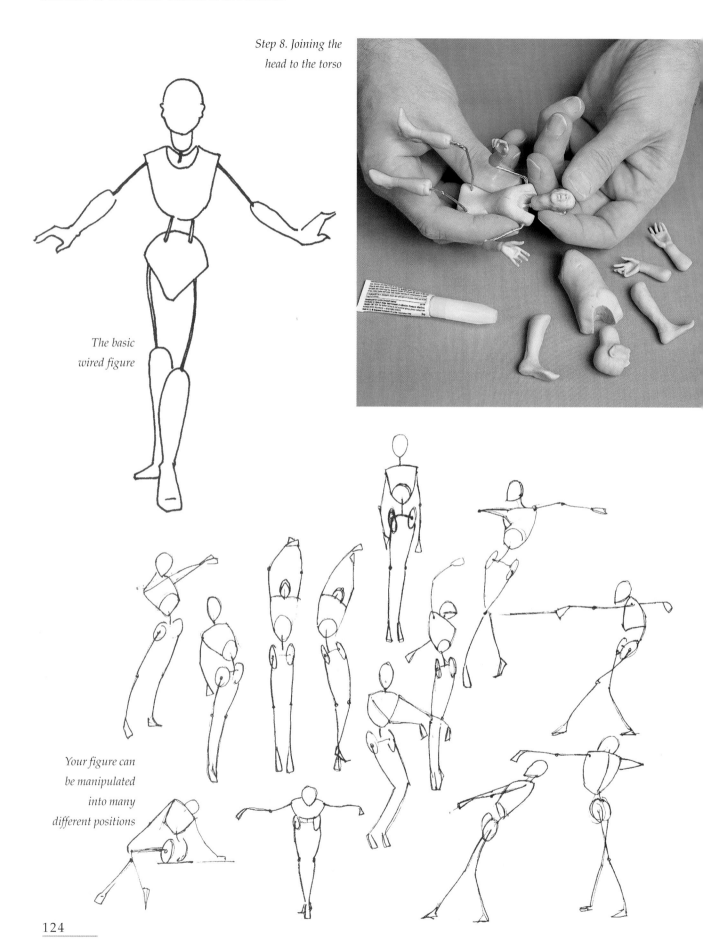

Step 8. Joining the head to the torso

The basic wired figure

Your figure can be manipulated into many different positions

6 Push two pins into the body part as before, and place onto the pelvis unit to mark. Remove the pins and make the holes for the wires.

7 Bake the figure in the oven in the normal way.

8 To make up the unit, cut longer wires than you need, then reassemble the figure. Join the head to the torso, then the torso to the pelvis, using the proportion chart as a guide.

9 Stuff the gaps with cotton wool and glue the neck padding in place. The waist may need a layer of fine cotton fabric to hold it in place. Glue this onto the clay.

FILLING IN THE LIMBS

Quite often you will need to show a bare arm or thigh. To sculpt the entire figure in one go is very difficult, due to the nature of the clay. However, the nature of the clay

gives us an added advantage; it can be baked over and over with no ill effects.

1 Make the units and bake as normal, but only wire on either the forearms or the legs. Of course you can do both of them, but why give yourself the trouble.

2 Pose the arms or legs into the position you want, and simply add on clay to fill in the area that you would normally wind with wool.

3 To get an absolutely perfect join between the baked and the unbaked clay is difficult; washing the join with acetone helps, or you could try modelling the new part a little proud and sanding down the join until smooth after baking. Practice will teach you the best way.

4 With the legs, it's important to check that the figure will stand easily before you bake it.

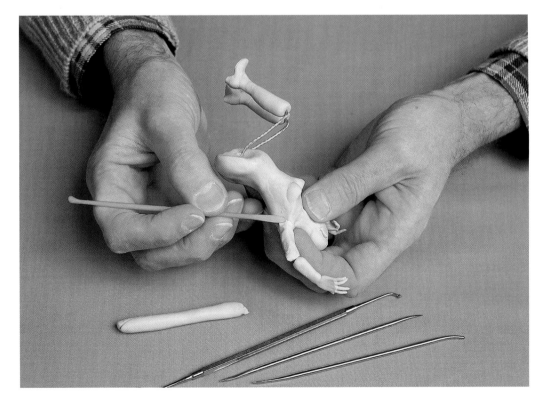

Step 2. Filling in with extra clay

5 Bake one part first, and then fill in the other area.

Once you have made a few figures and gained some confidence in the method of working, new possibilities for movement will become apparent. Suddenly, you will want to have your figure reaching or lifting, turning or twisting. The more complex wiring gives you the option to position the figure in most of these poses, but not all of them. When someone raises his or her arms above the head, the shoulders rise, too, and close in to each side of the head. In a figure, it would be *almost* possible to bend the wires upwards, but unfortunately, they would still want to go outwards, which means you would get a curved and slightly shortened arm. It is better to mount the wires into the figure downwards through the top of the shoulder.

PAINTING

1 First of all, brush a wash of colour onto the face and neck. Aquacolor No. 7W is excellent. I know it looks dark, but trust me, it works. Dip a large brush into the water and work it into the foundation cake until the brush is loaded, and slap it onto the face and neck, working the colour well into the cracks and creases. It's more important to get it there than onto the surface.

2 Wait a minute for the colour to set slightly, then wipe off most of it with a paper towel. If you're working on two figures, do this on one first and look at the difference. The unpainted one will have flat, ill-defined shadows, and the other will have a three-dimensional look. Don't panic if you get it wrong, you can always wash it off with soap and water.

Step 1. Painting the foundation colour onto the figure

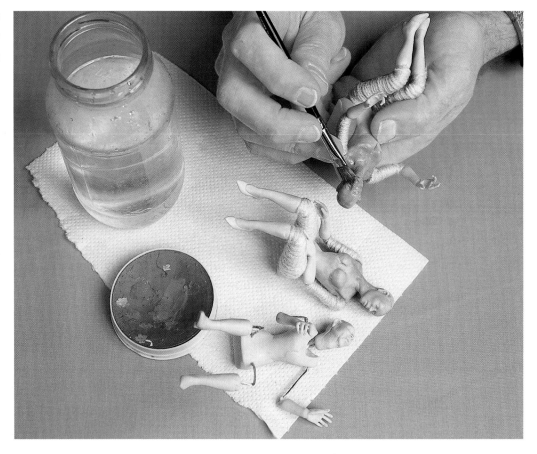

MATERIALS AND EQUIPMENT

AQUACOLOR FOUNDATION No. 7W (TAN)

AQUACOLOR FOUNDATION No. 075 (RED)

SOFT BRUSH TO APPLY FOUNDATION COLOUR

SABLE OR SYNTHETIC BRUSH No. 000

ACRYLIC PAINTS

PAPER TOWELS

WASHING-UP LIQUID

COTTON BUDS

3 If, instead of using Aquacolor, you decide you want to use acrylic paint, you must first prime the surface of the clay with a little washing-up liquid diluted with water. Unfortunately, some clays remain very oily even after baking, and following this method will help to neutralize it.

PAINTING THE FEATURES

This is the moment when you see the face appear. It may surprise you; be flexible and allow it to reveal itself. It might not be what you intended, but as long as you don't try to force it to be something it doesn't want to be, it will be fine. Remember that at any stage you can scrub it clean and start again. In fact, this is not a bad way to learn just what paint can do to transform one face into many.

(Warning: before you start to paint the features, remember it is a good idea to keep breathing!)

1 Paint the white of the eyes first, except they should never be painted white (unless you're doing a 'Lunatic Asylum' look) The eyelid and lashes create a shadow over the eyeball, so mix some white with the foundation colour to make a shade one stage lighter than the face, and paint in the

Step 1. Painting the white of the eyes

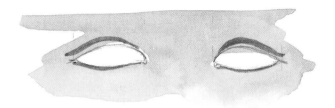

Step 2

Step 3

Step 4

Painting the eyes

3 Make up your chosen iris colour. Your brush will be overloaded with paint, so roll the hairs of the brush out of the paint puddle, leaving a trail of excess paint in its wake. This will unload the brush and sharpen the tip. Go back to the paint puddle, picking up a small amount on the tip, and paint in the irises. This is the point when you can correct the balance of the eyes. In a normal face, no matter how the eyes differ, the irises should always point in the same direction, unless you want a 'one eye in the pot and the other up the chimney' look. Only with looks of anger, surprise and sheer delight do the irises appear as a complete circle; most of the time they are only partly visible. Did you remember to breath?

4 Paint in the eyelash line, starting a third of the way in, from barely visible to a wider band at the outer edge. (If you start from the very inside of the eye you can end up with a cross-eyed look.) Use the same technique for picking up the paint as for the iris.

5 Paint in the pupil and when set, a minute or so later, take a very clean brush and add a highlight of pure white at the outer edge of the iris/pupil – don't go mad, it's very tiny.

6 To increase the depth of the eye even further, you may wish to add a brown shadow line at the outside of the crease line. This works particularly well on a male face and doesn't look as 'made up' as you might think.

7 Paint in the eyebrows, but before you start keep a cotton bud handy to wipe

eye. Don't panic if at this stage you find that the eyes are lopsided; in reality, eyes are never symmetrical. Paint from the corner of the eye to the middle, then turn the figure upside-down and repeat.

2 Take some Aquacolor No. 075, a sort of terracotta, and paint a crescent above the eye in the crease and into the inside socket, followed by a fine line underneath the eye. It will look very painterly at this stage, but don't worry, this is going to give life and depth to the finished eyes.

off any mistakes. The brows can alter a face in a surprising way and are often overlooked as just 'being there'. Try painting them on a piece of paper first until you get the style right.

8 Lips come in a million shapes and sizes, either natural or applied. For men, unless you're doing a period face where they were 'made up', a line of Aquacolor No. 075 in the crease is all that is needed. On the female face, it is best to start with a line of deep red between the lips before adding the lip colour, otherwise the mouth will appear flat. Remember that the light falls downwards and the upper lip is usually in shadow, so either paint the upper lip darker, or lighten the lower lip on the curve. A tiny pair of highlights on the finished lower lip will give added shape to the mouth.

9 Finally, using a cotton bud, add on cheek colour with some Aquacolour No. 075, fanning the colour out. To add even more shape to the face you can also colour the temples, the chin and the tips of the ears. For a boozy look, run this colour over the tip of the nose.

10 While you have the paints out, remember to tint the hands with some foundation colour.

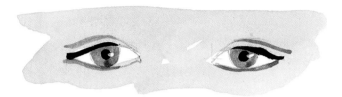

Step 5

Step 6

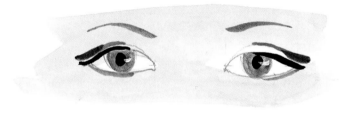

Step 7

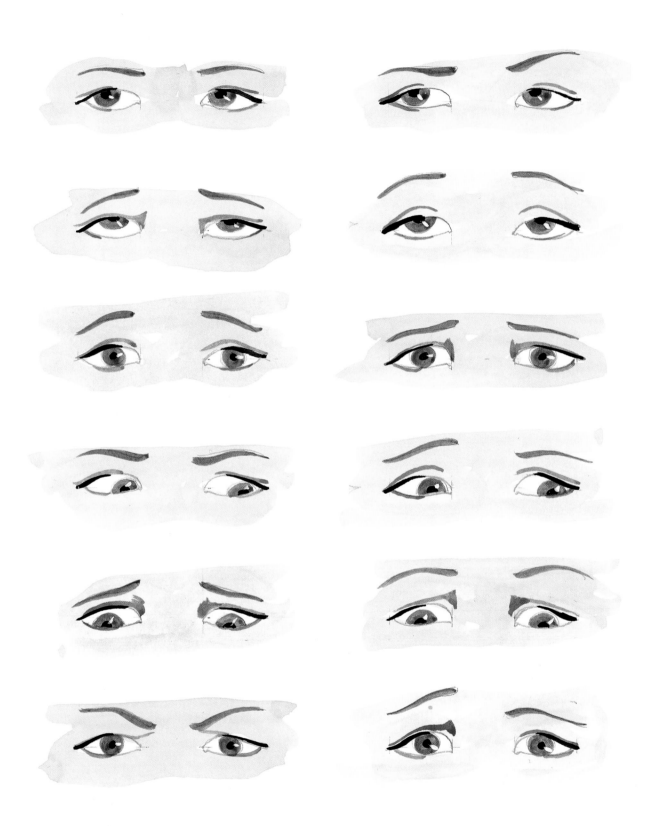

The same eye shape can be painted to give a wide variety of expressions

WIGGING

Here we get to the bit that many people find the most difficult. I think we all feel that someone else does it better. I look at some people's work and despair that I'll never be as good as them, but then I do that with many things, not just hair. Learn from other people by all means, but learn from yourself at the same time. If you buy enough hair in the first place, you can afford to rip the wig off if you're not happy, learning along the way what you did that didn't please you, not what you did wrong.

LADIES' WAVE HAIRSTYLE
This is one of the easiest possible hairstyles.

MATERIALS AND EQUIPMENT
·:·

HAIR

SPRAY STARCH OR HAIRSPRAY

GLUE IN SYRINGE

RUBBER MINI PLEATER (SMALL SIZE)

STRIP OF PLASTIC (FOR PUSHING THE HAIR)

CIGARETTE LIGHTER

ARTIST'S BRUSH

ACETONE

---

1 Take a hank of hair and spread out thinly to about 2cm (1in) wide and 12cm (5in) long. Spray it lightly with spray starch and press between your fingers to spread it through the hair.

2 Place one end on the mini pleater and press the first wave between the groove with the edge of the plastic (you can at last find a use for that store card you've never used). If you hold the hair over your fingers as you go, you can feed the hair into the subsequent grooves without pulling the previous one out (at least, that's the theory). The best bit is that you should not try to get them even or going in a straight line; the more haphazard, the more natural the end result. Isn't it nice to get good marks for not doing something perfectly?

3 Once the hair is in the pleater let it rest to dry. You will find that the hair takes up only a small amount of space, so if you like, you can keep on adding until it's full.

4 Once really dry, use the piece of plastic to remove it from the pleater, push from the side. Don't attempt to lift it out.

5 Tease the hair out slightly, unless of course you want to achieve a 'Maison Doreen' style perm (OAPs' cheap rate on Thursdays).

6 Glue one end of the wave strip onto the head in any place you think is right and twist and push the rest into a style suitable for the period. Once you have an idea of the look you want, lift it up from the head, spread some glue on the scalp and press into place.

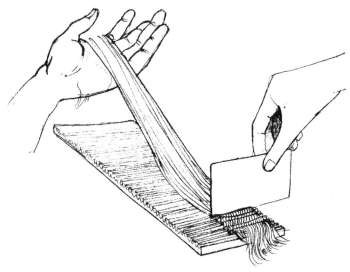

Step 2. Pressing hair into the mini pleater

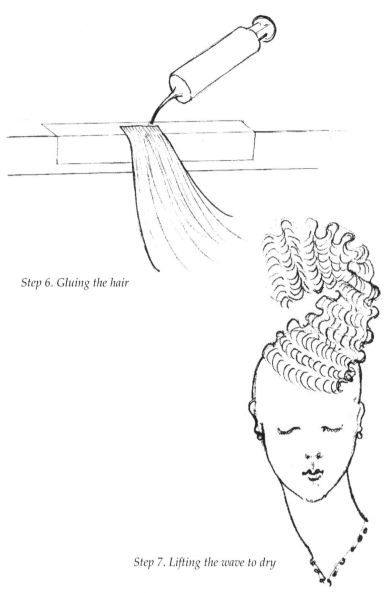

Step 6. Gluing the hair

Step 7. Lifting the wave to dry

7 To fix and add extra style, spray some starch into a small cup and when the foam subsides, dip a brush into the liquid and run a little between the waves. Before it dries completely, lift the waves with a pin to arrange in style.

8 Once dry, you may find those irritating wisps of hair sticking up. If you are very brave, you may try this. Take a cigarette lighter and whizz the head through the flame to singe the strays away. Beware, if it rests too long on the face, the clay will go bright green. Yes, I've done it!

A wash with acetone will remedy this, but you'll have to paint the face all over again.

Once you've had a go at this one, you'll find it quite simple to do a shorter version for men.

BUILT-UP HAIRSTYLES

MATERIALS AND EQUIPMENT

HAIR
SPRAY STARCH OR HAIRSPRAY
GLUE IN A SYRINGE
SHARP SCISSORS

1 Prepare your work area first. I find it best to use the edge of my worktable to glue on, but you can use a board. The glue will build up as you work, so it is best to run a strip of masking tape along this edge to rip off later.

2 Pull off a length of hair and spread it out to about 1in (25mm) wide. Spray lightly with hairspray if you are intending to do a conventional hairstyle, or spray starch if you want a rat-tail, greasy look.

3 Trim one end of the hair level and run a strip of glue along this end, working it well into the hair with the side of the syringe.

HAIRSTYLES WITH A PARTING

> ### MATERIALS AND EQUIPMENT
> ❖
>
> HAIR
> SPRAY STARCH OR HAIRSPRAY
> KNITTING NEEDLE OR THIN LENGTH OF WIRE
> GLUE IN A SYRINGE
> A PIN
> CIGARETTE LIGHTER
> ARTIST'S BRUSH

1 Spread some glue over the back of the head, then place the strip of hair over the same part of the head above the nape of the neck. Trim the hair off, leaving a generous length.

2 Glue the hair again, and add another strip above this.

3 Repeat over each side of the head. Your head should now resemble a long-haired monk's tonsure with a bald patch on top.

4 Prepare another strip, and run a line of glue on one side of the top of the head.

5 Place the strip of hair on this, and pat into place. Dig the tip of your fingernail along the edge of the glue line of the hair to define the parting and fold back the hair into place.

6 Repeat this to make the other side of the parting.

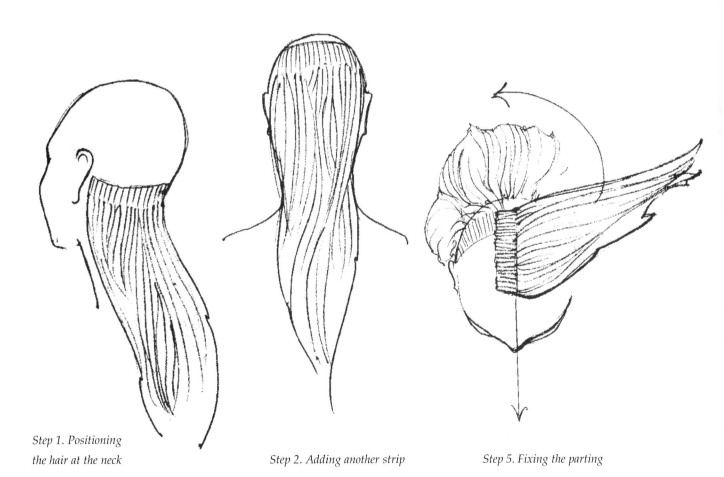

Step 1. Positioning the hair at the neck

Step 2. Adding another strip

Step 5. Fixing the parting

7 Once you are certain that the glue is set, take a pin and 'comb' the hair into its position.

8 For 'ratty' hair, spray some starch into a cup, paint the liquid starch onto the hair, and arrange .

9 To curl the ends of a conventional hairstyle, take a knitting needle, comb the hair back and roll the hair onto the needle. To fix the curl, run a lighter up and down the roll of hair.

HAIRSTYLES WITH A PARTING AND A FRINGE

1 Glue the hair into place as before until you get to the tonsured look.

2 Make a fringe. Glue a strip of hair as you have been doing, but this time pinch the glued part to form a point, allowing the hair to fan out slightly.

MATERIALS AND EQUIPMENT

HAIR
SPRAY STARCH OR HAIRSPRAY
KNITTING NEEDLE OR THIN LENGTH OF WIRE
GLUE IN A SYRINGE
CIGARETTE LIGHTER
ARTIST'S BRUSH
SHARP SCISSORS

---

3 To curl the fringe, bend the hair over a knitting needle as before and use the lighter to fix it.

4 Place on top of the head and glue in position. Trim off, leaving a generous length of hair to trim later on.

5 Glue on the parting of the hair as previously instructed.

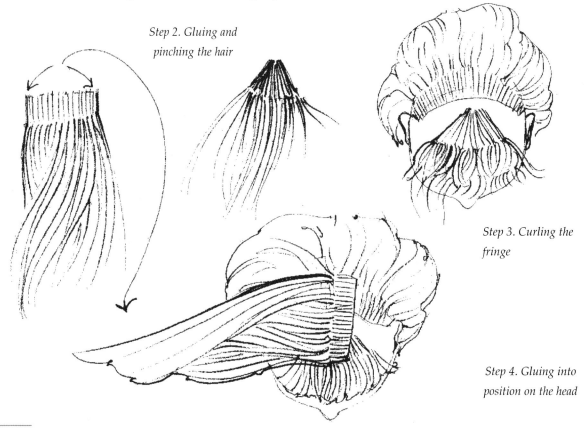

Step 2. Gluing and pinching the hair

Step 3. Curling the fringe

Step 4. Gluing into position on the head

UPSWEPT BACKSTYLE I

For this style, simply reverse the two back strips of hair.

1 Glue the back of the crown first, with the hair going upwards.

2 Next, glue the hair at the nape of the neck.

These very basic hairstyles, once you have practised them a few times, will provide you the foundations for trying many more elaborate styles. If you have been generous with the length of your piece of hair, you will find it quite straightforward to twist the hair up into all sorts of fashionable period looks.

UPSWEPT BACK STYLE II

1 Glue a strip of hair over the front hairline and fold back.

2 Add a wad of teased hair to lift up the front of the hair.

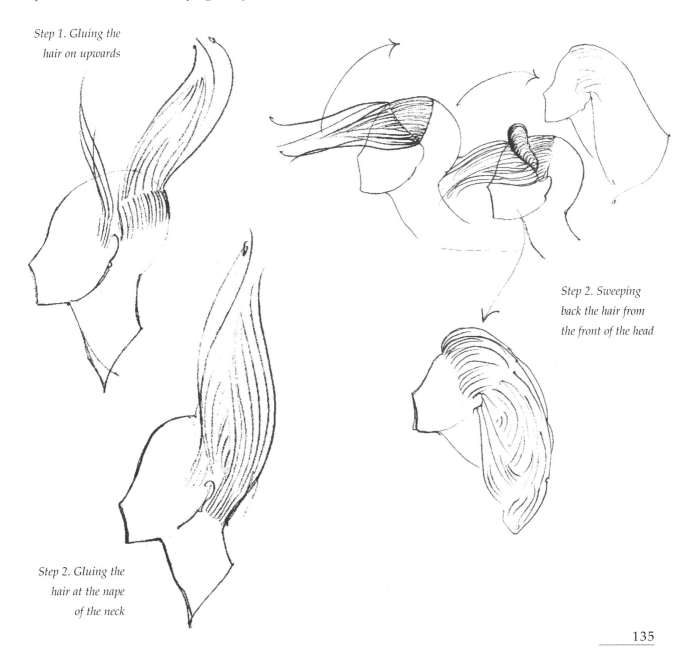

Step 1. Gluing the hair on upwards

Step 2. Sweeping back the hair from the front of the head

Step 2. Gluing the hair at the nape of the neck

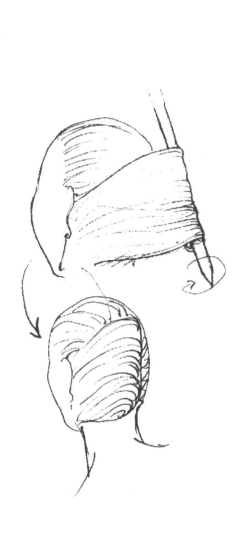

Step 2. Rolling the hair into a pleat with the use of a knitting needle

Step 1. Twisting the hair into a top knot

FRENCH PLEAT

1 Comb one side of the hair across the back of the head and glue into place.

2 Place the other side of the hair over your knitting needle and roll it into its position.

TOP KNOT

1 Glue one end of a generous length of hair to the head, and twist tightly until it begins to knot against itself.

2 Glue the top knot into place very firmly so that it cannot untwist.

ADDING EXTRA HAIRPIECES TO YOUR STYLE

Remember that many of the fashionable ladies during various periods have used 'bought hair', so adding extra hair to your basic style is quite correct.

MATERIALS AND EQUIPMENT

HAIR

SPRAY STARCH OR HAIRSPRAY

KNITTING NEEDLE OR THIN LENGTH OF WIRE
(IN A RANGE OF THICKNESSES)

GLUE IN A SYRINGE

CIGARETTE LIGHTER

ARTIST'S BRUSH

SHARP SCISSORS

RINGLETS AND OTHER CURLED STYLES

1 Take a very fine length of hair and spray it lightly with hairspray.

2 Wind it around and along a knitting needle or thin wire.

3 To fix, take a lighter and run it up and down the needle.

4 Slide it off the needle and use in your hairstyle as desired.

5 Cut lengths bunched together to form ringlets, but you can also glue one end onto the basic hairstyle and push and twist the length of curl into all sorts of attractive styles, gluing as you go.

Step 2. Curling the hair with a knitting needle

Step 2. Fixing the ends

Step 1. Plaiting the hair

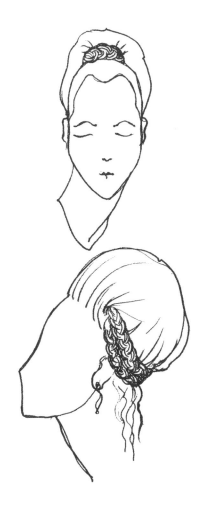

Step 3. Working into the hair

PLAITS

1 Take three fine strips of hair and spray with hairspray to hold them.

2 Fix the three ends of the hair together, attaching this end to something you can pull against.

3 Plait the strands together. You can also enhance this effect by using an additional length of gilded embroidery silk or ribbon.

SHORT CURLY HAIR

1 Make more ringlet lengths than you think you will need and chop them up into small pieces.

2 Glue the figure's head within the hairline and pile on the curls, pressing them onto the glue, lightly but firmly.

3 To hold this style together, spray either starch or hairspray into a cup and gently wet the hair using a small brush.

4 Lift the curls while still wet, and leave to dry.

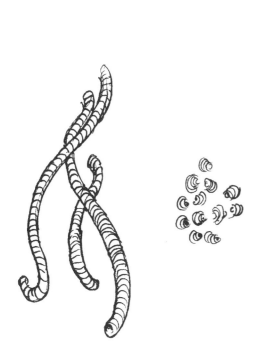

Step 1. Making lengths of ringlets

Step 2. Piling the curls onto the head

MEN'S SHORT CROP STYLE

This style is one of the easiest to complete and very effective.

1 Take a bunch of hair and, with a pair of very sharp scissors, clip off approximately ⅛ in (3mm) tufts until you have a big pile of flock; you will need more than you think.

MATERIALS AND EQUIPMENT

HAIR

SPRAY STARCH OR HAIRSPRAY

KNITTING NEEDLE OR THIN LENGTH OF WIRE

GLUE IN A SYRINGE

ARTIST'S BRUSH

SHARP SCISSORS

RUBBER MINI PLEATER (SMALL SIZE)

STRIP OF PLASTIC (FOR PUSHING THE HAIR)

2 Glue the figure's head within the hairline and push chunks of flock onto it, brushing off any excess as you go. Don't worry if you get bald bits, just add some more glue and flock again. (Hey-ho, we've done Magwich.)

CENTRE-PARTED HAIR

Centre-parted hair is worked in exactly the same way as for the ladies' style, and then trimmed to a fashionable length.

SIDE-PARTED HAIR

1 Work the back of the style and over the ears as you did for the ladies' hairstyle worn down.

2 To get a 'swept back' side, glue a strip as normal, but trim the glued edge very close to the free hair.

Step 1. Working the back of the style

Step 2. Creating the swept back look

Step 3. Fixing the length of parting hair

Step 6. Arranging the hair into place

3 Glue the head at the temples, and place the strip of hair in a curvy line with the hair going over the ear. Repeat this on the other side.

4 Trim this to the length of the back hair. It'll stick up at first; don't worry the starch will put paid to that.

5 Glue on one parting strip over the other side of the head.

6 Wet the hair with the liquid starch, and arrange into place.

Play with these styles, and you will find that they form the basis for as many styles as you wish.

DRESSING THE FIGURE

Now that you have finished your figure, it's time to dress it. Take a moment to actually see what you have created. Quite often I will start out with a strong idea about how the figure should look, and then I will be surprised by how the figure speaks to me in quite a different way. For example, a very elegant lady in my imagination turns out to be 'no better than she should be', and no amount of lace and silk will disguise it.

The guidelines that follow are intended to offer you both advice, and to start you thinking about period style. I have not exhausted by any means all there is to say about costuming your figure, but with some reading, imagination and a little skill, you are well on your way to costuming your figure.

Scrooge and Marley's Ghost from Dickens' A Christmas Carol, dressed to period.

To many doll makers, the idea of making clothes, even in miniature, raises the spectre of school sewing classes – all that tiresome basting. Of course, today, modern glues and iron-on hem gauze save the drudgery of sewing everything by hand. So, don't be intimidated by the work!

FABRICS, NEEDLES AND THREADS

Use natural fabrics and test them out in the shop for 'creasability'. Twist the corner of the fabric between your fingers, and if it creases well, choose that one. Good stores will label the fibre content of their fabrics, but many modern silks are crease-resistant, so beware. Always avoid anything with the dreaded polyester woven into it; in my opinion, it's not a fabric, it's an insult to the dressmaker.

Only select good quality, fine needles. Look for Sharps Nos. 8, 9 and 10. They are short and have a small eye that enables you to pull the thread through your fabric without tearing the weave.

Present-day sewing thread is most often synthetic and intended for a sewing machine. The thread is twisted the wrong way for sewing by hand and can knot as you work, but there are ways to polish the thread which enables you to thread it more easily. If you can find them, old books on embroidery advise you to wax the thread before cutting it from the spool. I have tried this and find that it can make the thread sticky. It also has a tendency to pull out of the needle. Instead, try running the thread over a bar of soap, and always use the thread end farthest from the reel rather than the severed end.

As you work, remember to keep the spray starch handy, and use it to stiffen the fabric before you cut it, and if you want to add drape later on.

CHOOSING A PERIOD STYLE

When choosing the style and period of dress for your figure, don't worry too much about the detail at first. Instead, concentrate on the silhouette. Do some research on the period and character you would like your figure to reflect. Go to a museum or historic property to see if they have any costumes, or the library for books on fashion of the period to find out about the styles for men and women, and the way clothes were padded, boned and secured together.

If you are making a group of figures of different ages, it's better to dress the older characters in a slightly earlier period dress than the younger ones. This will look more authentic, because each generation dresses in the fashion of its own moment. Also, the upper classes had their clothes specially tailored for them in limited quantities, and 'off the peg' clothes were not available until the late nineteenth century. In contrast, the lower classes wore second- or third-hand clothes, and the poor tended to make do with what they had, often repairing the same garments until they were threadbare. So, don't feel you have to be slavish to the period. Your dress should approximately reflect the style of your room setting, but a little imagination and artistic licence also lends your work its own personality, and makes it unique.

Good luck!

ABOUT THE AUTHOR

JAMES CARRINGTON trained at Nottingham College of Art and went on to specialize in theatre design. Now a full-time doll-maker, James's work is exhibited in museums and in private collections around the world. He also lectures on figure making and organizes occasional workshops from his home in London.

He has recently been granted the prestigious status of Artisan in the category of Figures by the International Guild of Miniature Artisans Ltd (IGMA).

INDEX

GMC Publications

BOOKS

WOODCARVING

The Art of the Woodcarver	GMC Publications
Carving Architectural Detail in Wood:	
The Classical Tradition	Frederick Wilbur
Carving Birds & Beasts	GMC Publications
Carving Nature: Wildlife Studies in Wood	Frank Fox-Wilson
Carving on Turning	Chris Pye
Carving Realistic Birds	David Tippey
Decorative Woodcarving	Jeremy Williams
Elements of Woodcarving	Chris Pye
Essential Tips for Woodcarvers	GMC Publications
Essential Woodcarving Techniques	Dick Onians
Further Useful Tips for Woodcarvers	GMC Publications
Lettercarving in Wood: A Practical Course	Chris Pye
Making & Using Working Drawings for	
Realistic Model Animals	Basil Fordham
Power Tools for Woodcarving	David Tippey
Practical Tips for Turners & Carvers	GMC Publications
Relief Carving in Wood: A Practical Introduction	Chris Pye
Understanding Woodcarving	GMC Publications
Understanding Woodcarving in the Round	GMC Publications
Useful Techniques for Woodcarvers	GMC Publications
Wildfowl Carving – Volume 1	Jim Pearce
Wildfowl Carving – Volume 2	Jim Pearce
The Woodcarvers	GMC Publications
Woodcarving: A Complete Course	Ron Butterfield
Woodcarving: A Foundation Course	Zoë Gertner
Woodcarving for Beginners	GMC Publications
Woodcarving Tools & Equipment Test Reports	GMC Publications
Woodcarving Tools, Materials & Equipment	Chris Pye

WOODTURNING

Adventures in Woodturning	David Springett
Bert Marsh: Woodturner	Bert Marsh
Bill Jones' Notes from the Turning Shop	Bill Jones
Bill Jones' Further Notes from the Turning Shop	Bill Jones
Bowl Turning Techniques Masterclass	Tony Boase
Colouring Techniques for Woodturners	Jan Sanders
The Craftsman Woodturner	Peter Child
Decorative Techniques for Woodturners	Hilary Bowen
Faceplate Turning	GMC Publications

Fun at the Lathe	R.C. Bell
Further Useful Tips for Woodturners	GMC Publications
Illustrated Woodturning Techniques	John Hunnex
Intermediate Woodturning Projects	GMC Publications
Keith Rowley's Woodturning Projects	Keith Rowley
Multi-Centre Woodturning	Ray Hopper
Practical Tips for Turners & Carvers	GMC Publications
Spindle Turning	GMC Publications
Turning Green Wood	Michael O'Donnell
Turning Miniatures in Wood	John Sainsbury
Turning Pens and Pencils	Kip Christensen & Rex Burningham
Turning Wooden Toys	Terry Lawrence
Understanding Woodturning	Ann & Bob Phillips
Useful Techniques for Woodturners	GMC Publications
Useful Woodturning Projects	GMC Publications
Woodturning: Bowls, Platters, Hollow Forms, Vases,	
Vessels, Bottles, Flasks, Tankards, Plates	GMC Publications
Woodturning: A Foundation Course	
(New Edition)	Keith Rowley
Woodturning: A Fresh Approach	Robert Chapman
Woodturning: An Individual Approach	Dave Regester
Woodturning: A Source Book of Shapes	John Hunnex
Woodturning Jewellery	Hilary Bowen
Woodturning Masterclass	Tony Boase
Woodturning Techniques	GMC Publications
Woodturning Tools & Equipment Test Reports	GMC Publications
Woodturning Wizardry	David Springett

WOODWORKING

Bird Boxes and Feeders for the Garden	Dave Mackenzie
Complete Woodfinishing	Ian Hosker
David Charlesworth's Furniture-Making Techniques	
	David Charlesworth
Furniture & Cabinetmaking Projects	GMC Publications
Furniture-Making Projects for the Wood Craftsman	
	GMC Publications
Furniture-Making Techniques for the Wood Craftsman	
	GMC Publications
Furniture Projects	Rod Wales
Furniture Restoration (Practical Crafts)	Kevin Jan Bonner
Furniture Restoration and Repair	
for Beginners	Kevin Jan Bonner

Furniture Restoration Workshop	*Kevin Jan Bonner*
Green Woodwork	*Mike Abbott*
Making & Modifying Woodworking Tools	*Jim Kingshott*
Making Chairs and Tables	*GMC Publications*
Making Classic English Furniture	*Paul Richardson*
Making Fine Furniture	*Tom Darby*
Making Little Boxes from Wood	*John Bennett*
Making Shaker Furniture	*Barry Jackson*
Making Woodwork Aids and Devices	*Robert Wearing*
Minidrill: Fifteen Projects	*John Everett*
Pine Furniture Projects for the Home	*Dave Mackenzie*
Router Magic: Jigs, Fixtures and Tricks to Unleash your Router's Full Potential	*Bill Hylton*
Routing for Beginners	*Anthony Bailey*
Scrollsaw Pattern Book	*John Everett*
The Scrollsaw: Twenty Projects	*John Everett*
Sharpening: The Complete Guide	*Jim Kingshott*
Sharpening Pocket Reference Book	*Jim Kingshott*
Space-Saving Furniture Projects	*Dave Mackenzie*
Stickmaking: A Complete Course	*Andrew Jones & Clive George*
Stickmaking Handbook	*Andrew Jones & Clive George*
Test Reports: *The Router* and *Furniture & Cabinetmaking*	*GMC Publications*
Veneering: A Complete Course	*Ian Hosker*
Woodfinishing Handbook (Practical Crafts)	*Ian Hosker*
Woodworking with the Router: Professional Router Techniques any Woodworker can Use	*Bill Hylton & Fred Matlack*
The Workshop	*Jim Kingshott*

UPHOLSTERY

Seat Weaving (Practical Crafts)	*Ricky Holdstock*
The Upholsterer's Pocket Reference Book	*David James*
Upholstery: A Complete Course (Revised Edition)	*David James*
Upholstery Restoration	*David James*
Upholstery Techniques & Projects	*David James*
Upholstery Tips and Hints	*David James*

TOYMAKING

Designing & Making Wooden Toys	*Terry Kelly*
Fun to Make Wooden Toys & Games	*Jeff & Jennie Loader*
Making Wooden Toys & Games	*Jeff & Jennie Loader*
Restoring Rocking Horses	*Clive Green & Anthony Dew*
Scrollsaw Toy Projects	*Ivor Carlyle*
Scrollsaw Toys for All Ages	*Ivor Carlyle*
Wooden Toy Projects	*GMC Publications*

DOLLS' HOUSES AND MINIATURES

Architecture for Dolls' Houses	*Joyce Percival*
A Beginners' Guide to the Dolls' House Hobby	*Jean Nisbett*
The Complete Dolls' House Book	*Jean Nisbett*
The Dolls' House 1/24 Scale: A Complete Introduction	*Jean Nisbett*
Dolls' House Accessories, Fixtures and Fittings	*Andrea Barham*
Dolls' House Bathrooms: Lots of Little Loos	*Patricia King*
Dolls' House Fireplaces and Stoves	*Patricia King*
Easy to Make Dolls' House Accessories	*Andrea Barham*
Heraldic Miniature Knights	*Peter Greenhill*
Make Your Own Dolls' House Furniture	*Maurice Harper*
Making Dolls' House Furniture	*Patricia King*
Making Georgian Dolls' Houses	*Derek Rowbottom*
Making Miniature Gardens	*Freida Gray*
Making Miniature Oriental Rugs & Carpets	*Meik & Ian McNaughton*
Making Period Dolls' House Accessories	*Andrea Barham*
Making 1/12 Scale Character Figures	*James Carrington*
Making Tudor Dolls' Houses	*Derek Rowbottom*
Making Victorian Dolls' House Furniture	*Patricia King*
Miniature Bobbin Lace	*Roz Snowden*
Miniature Embroidery for the Georgian Dolls' House	*Pamela Warner*
Miniature Embroidery for the Victorian Dolls' House	*Pamela Warner*
Miniature Needlepoint Carpets	*Janet Granger*
More Miniature Oriental Rugs & Carpets	*Meik & Ian McNaughton*
The Secrets of the Dolls' House Makers	*Jean Nisbett*

CRAFTS

American Patchwork Designs in Needlepoint	*Melanie Tacon*
A Beginners' Guide to Rubber Stamping	*Brenda Hunt*
Blackwork: A New Approach	*Brenda Day*
Celtic Cross Stitch Designs	*Carol Phillipson*
Celtic Knotwork Designs	*Sheila Sturrock*
Celtic Knotwork Handbook	*Sheila Sturrock*
Celtic Spirals and Other Designs	*Sheila Sturrock*
Collage from Seeds, Leaves and Flowers	*Joan Carver*
Complete Pyrography	*Stephen Poole*
Contemporary Smocking	*Dorothea Hall*
Creating Colour with Dylon	*Dylon International*
Creating Knitwear Designs	*Pat Ashforth & Steve Plummer*
Creative Doughcraft	*Patricia Hughes*
Creative Embroidery Techniques Using Colour Through Gold	*Daphne J. Ashby & Jackie Woolsey*

GARDENING

VIDEOS

MAGAZINES

WOODTURNING ◆ WOODCARVING
FURNITURE & CABINETMAKING
THE DOLLS' HOUSE MAGAZINE
THE ROUTER ◆ BUSINESSMATTERS
◆ WATER GARDENING ◆ EXOTIC
GARDENING ◆ OUTDOOR
PHOTOGRAPHY ◆ WOODWORKING
GARDEN CALENDAR

The above represents a full list of all titles currently published or scheduled to be published.

All are available direct from the Publishers or through bookshops, newsagents and specialist retailers.

To place an order, or to obtain a complete catalogue, contact:

**GMC Publications,
Castle Place, 166 High Street, Lewes,
East Sussex BN7 1XU, United
Kingdom
Tel: 01273 488005 Fax: 01273 478606
email: pubs@thegmcgroup.com**

Orders by credit card are accepted